13 Moons

Fiona Walker-Craven

ignotus press

First published in Great Britain by
ignotus press in 2002

© Fiona Walker-Craven (2002)

All rights reserved. The book is sold subject to the conditions that it shall not, by way of trade or otherwise, be re-lent, re-sold, hired out or otherwise circulated without the publisher's prior consent in any form of binding or cover other than that in which it is published and without a similar condition including this condition being imposed on the subsequent purchaser. No part of this publication may be reproduced, stored in a retrieval system, or transmitted in any form or by any means, electronic, mechanical, photocopying, recording or otherwise, without prior permission of the publishers and copyright holders.

Website: www.ignotuspress.com

British Library Cataloguing in Publication Data
ISBN: 1 903768 02 0

Edited by Claire Maguire
Printed in Great Britain by A2 Reprographics
Set in Baskerville Old Face 11pt

Contents

The Water Tide
January—The Wolf Moon 11

The Earth Tides
February—The Storm Moon 23
March-The Chaste Moon 29
April-The Seed Moon 37

The Fire Tides
May-The Hare Moon 47
June-The Honey Moon 57
July-The Mead Moon 69

The Air Tides
August-The Wort Moon 79
September-The Barley Moon 91
October— The Blood Moon 99

The Water Tides
November—The Snow Moon 109
December-The Oak Moon 115

The Thirteenth Moon 121

Epilogue 123

Pathworking 126

About the author

Although having worked her way through the coven system of traditional British Old Craft, the author still feels at heart that she is a *natural* witch, rather than a 'team-player'.

Writing as Fiona Walker-Craven, she focuses on the rural aspects of natural craft rather than "churning out yet another book giving the stereotypical workings of a coven, of which there are too many already".

Born and bred in Yorkshire, she comes from an old farming family and still prefers working out of doors, regardless of the weather. Having said that, she has just completed her second book, *High Rise Witch*, that caters for those who are unable to get out and meet Nature face to face — especially those who are disabled or who live in the inner towns and cities. Her new titles *Grymalkyn — Feline Magical Lore* and *Hearth Fire* are in the research stages.

Foreword:

When is a Witch not a Witch?

Good, plain old-fashioned traditional British Witchcraft is a *natural* ability rather than an acquired belief. It is being able to draw on that indefinable inner 'power' or energy that has been with an individual since birth, for a true Witch *is* born not made.

13 Moons is a fascinating book because Fiona Walker-Craven goes with the natural tides and changing seasons, according to Nature rather than any established calendar. Her spring ritual is timed to coincide with the flowering of the may (hawthorn) rather than some misaligned Celtic festival, or an official Bank Holiday. Autumn comes when the air is perfumed with that indescribable fragrance which is instantly recognised and never forgotten. Her 'wheel of the year' takes us on a strangely familiar journey through the woods and along hedgerows where age-old secrets and magic can still be discovered. This is Witchcraft as it was before it became the province of role-playing and the acquisition of rank.

On an inner note, this will be an enlightening book for those who have always felt they were, in some way different, and yet found no solace in the established modern traditions. *13 Moons* shows that it is not enough to want to be a Witch; the seeker must be prepared to live as a Witch — every day for the rest of his or her life. The comfort is discovering that you are not alone ...

Mélusine Draco

Introduction

It has certainly been with a good deal of thought and some degree of trepidation that I have been persuaded to reveal some of the thoughts and practices of a *natural* witch. This reluctance to divulge such 'truths' does not stem from a misguided attempt to protect any so-called ancient tradition, because everything which has been allegedly recorded and remembered has already been revealed. My reluctance is purely personal and comes from an inner fear of revealing too much of *myself.*

Nowadays, the pagan press is full of advertisements from groups and neo-magical orders, all willing to reveal the 'greater mysteries' to anyone with enough money to pay for them. Yet the one universal truth that they all avoid disclosing is that no single system or tradition can possibly teach you everything. It stands to reason that the world, the universe and the mysteries of the spirit, are far too complex for the average human being to grasp in one short lifetime. Indeed, most of us will consider ourselves fortunate if we can occasionally catch a fleeting glimpse. Nevertheless, my aim is to offer inspiration to those individuals who know deep within themselves that they neither need, nor want to join, any established modern tradition.

The natural witch senses these 'hidden' things, and it is instinct that encourages us to seek out and hone those ancient skills. We are self-driven and spiritually guided through life by something we 'know' and inexplicably recognise. *For this* reason, the natural witch has no need of formal groups with their rules and regulations, for we are governed by Nature's rules, that are imposed on every member of humanity. When we bring man-made rules into the equation we merely complicate matters for ourselves.

Unfortunately, in modern paganism it has become desirable to impress others with lists of achievement equating with exam results, and sadly, the term 'natural witch' seems to have somehow become relegated to something resembling second best. There are no, and never have been, degrees or titles for the natural witch. Those bearing titles bestowed within established groups and traditions are often short-sighted enough to presume that a natural witch's abilities are somewhat inferior. To those individuals I would say how wrong can you be.

No doubt I will also upset people by stating quite categorically that the vast majority who claim to be carrying on an ancient tradition are fooling themselves. Having more years than I care to admit under my cord, I can honestly say that for most, it is a clear case of making it up as they go along, until they eventually formulate a system that the gullible and inexperienced accept as genuine.

Far be it for me to say that some degree of development *cannot* be achieved by joining an established group, but the underlying problem with most, is that they make good use of the veil of illusion. Those laws which they will swear have come direct from the old gods themselves, have obviously been tainted with a very *human-*style interference. Much of what is passed off as being traditional witchcraft is actually a catalogue of man-made fantasies that are the by-products of other people's egos.

The real aim of *13 Moons* is to give people the confidence to go it alone; to learn a whole new set of values and to free themselves from the restrictions imposed by many modern Craft 'gurus'. Deep down, almost everyone has the ability to break free and there is no finer reward than the certainty that comes in knowing that you, and you alone, have discovered the path to the Old Ones. This is not to say that you are going to be the *only* one who has found their way, but if you can achieve this without the influence of others, you at least will know for certain that you are truly following the destiny which is right for you.

In order to break things down to basics, I have used the wheel of the year as our outline. Wherever we live in the world, the cycle of the year unfolds *naturally* regardless of what the human race may be doing; this can be equated to being the first 'magical truth'. The truth is always a good place to start and as we progress through the seasons the only thing you ever need to remember is that in being true to yourself, you are indeed honouring the Old Ones.

Sometimes, as we progress, we may discover that what we once believed wholeheartedly to be true, is no longer right for us. This does not matter: it was right at the time and that is what counts. It is natural and healthy to question ourselves, to change and grow - *as long as we do it honestly.* Because what we are really striving for is a healthy, confident growth of the spirit, and this can only truly be achieved when we are genuinely in tune with our gods.

The old gods of the witches do not speak to everyone. For many people these same universal truths will be discovered through other faiths and again, this is normal and right. Never fall into the trap of believing that because you have had a genuine magical or mystical experience that has revealed the Mysteries to you, that yours is the only truth.

Keep these gems of the Mysteries to yourself; never profane them or they may well be lost to you forever. Above all, do not be tempted to think that this means you are ready to become a teacher. Remember that old ego lurking in the shadows - it may well turn out to be the first *real* demon you will ever encounter.

The path of the natural witch is no less dramatic, awe-inspiring and inspired than that of the greatest magicians. Perhaps we simply know how to treasure these things in secrecy and in the time honoured way of the most secretive of all — the Ol' Lass herself.

Fiona Walker Craven
Yorkshire 2002

When icicles hang by the wall,
And Dick the shepherd, blows his nail,
And Tom bears logs into the hall,
And milk comes frozen home in pail
When blood is nipp'd and ways be foul,
Then nightly sings the staring owl
    Love's Labour's Lost, William Shakespeare

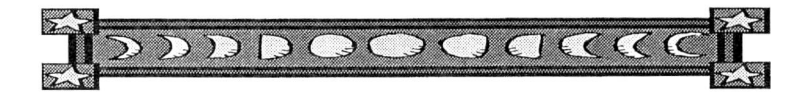

THE WATER TIDE
January—The Wolf Moon

I have chosen to use these names for the moons simply because they are old and very beautiful. If, however, we take time to think about each name in turn we begin to unravel many of the simple 'truths' in nature that have become shrouded in mystery.

It seems a travesty that our remote ancestors are portrayed as being somewhat less intelligent than people today. This is a strange way of looking at things when we consider that they could read the maps of the stars, chart the leys, divine the future and understand the power in herbs and plants. Today, the majority cannot even tell which phase the moon is in without referring to a calendar.

To appreciate the world of the natural witch, it is a good idea to set ourselves some time each day or night to simply watch what is going on around us in the natural world. If we can devote enough time to jotting down our findings then so much the better, because it is amazing how useful these notes will be in the years to come. What we are doing is creating what, in some circles, has become popularly known as a 'book of shadows'.

As well as remembering the old names for each of the moons, we could also think about the way the different seasons came to be recognised as being in harmony with the four elements of earth, water, air and fire. For over a hundred years these tides have been presented in books as:

Spring : Fire
Summer : Water
Autumn : Air
Winter : Earth

It must be remembered, however, that these tables come to us via the ritual magic traditions, many of which came from the East. No doubt these correspondences are perfectly compatible in Eastern mysticism from the *southern* hemisphere, but if we compare them to the climate in the northern hemisphere, we can see that they do not align to our seasons. For the natural witch, the year is divided to coincide with the solstices and equinoxes, as follows:

November, December, January in the Water Tide (Winter)
February, March, April in the Earth Tide (Spring)
May, June, July in the Fire Tide (Summer)
August, September, October in the Air Tide (Autumn)

Although we begin with the Wolf Moon, this actually falls at the end of the Water Tide since, as with most aspects of natural magic, the changeover of these elemental tides cannot be pinned down to a specific date in the calendar. For just as the seasons make a gradual changeover, so do the elemental tides. On the first day of February we will not be likely to feel an abrupt shift into the Earth Tide, but we should be aware of those subtle changes that are taking place as we move towards it.

January, or the Wolf Moon, is an ideal starting point on the annual cycle because it is a quiet tide; a time of sitting by the hearth, keeping warm and safe. The old Anglo-Saxon name of Wolf Moon probably came about because at this time of year, when food was scarce and the snows lay heavy, the wolves were hungry enough to become bolder and more dangerous. They would prey on the perimeter of the settlements, desperate enough to take any living thing which strayed into their path.

A hungry animal will use all its skill and cunning, and a hungry pack will combine all these skills to work as a team in order to ensure the group's survival. It would not take long for our ancestors to make the connection between a pack of wolves and a group of people. Each has its ways of working together in unison, each has a social structure which keeps order, and each has its outcasts or renegades, who will not support the group.

For as long as there has been folk-lore and story-tellers, the wolf has been seen as having supernatural abilities, and maybe this is one reason why it has been chosen so often as a totem animal. There are many attributes in the wolf which make it a popular choice but there are other subtler qualities which are worthy of consideration. Later on I will go into more detail about totem animals, but for now let's begin at the beginning ...

For many, the main reason for not getting too deeply involved with witchcraft is a fear that something frightening will happen. This is a valid doubt and only a fool would leap into magical realms without first being certain that they will come to no harm. Of course, it is impossible to say that we will never experience something which unnerves us, but with correct preparations and a sound understanding about protection, it is reasonably safe to assume that we are unlikely to come to grief.

The greatest danger can come from other humans, but as the natural witch is more likely to work alone, this problem is effectively eliminated. It is not for nothing that one of the oldest witch sayings is: "Trust none!"

It is at this gateway into the unknown that we can equate ourselves with the Wolf Moon. The year is young and, in magical terms, so are we — and the new year stretches out before us full of unknown possibilities We accept there are hidden dangers but at the same time we know that if we take precautions to safeguard ourselves we stand a good chance of walking the path of the natural witch without danger.

One of the strongest messages of the Wolf Moon is of the need for protection - and we can take this to mean *magical* protection. It should be born in mind when looking at these old names that they must be viewed on two separate levels. On one hand, there is the practical reference to the physical world, while on another, less tangible level there are the magical influences which surround us. It is these magical influences which interest us and it will soon become apparent just how interwoven these are with the natural or physical world.

Assuming that you have no previous experience of working

magic (other than to have felt a stirring of the blood that comes upon you when you have been casually walking through the woods, or even just cutting through the park on a spring morning), let's begin by tackling those hidden fears we discussed earlier.

The most common and understandable fear among would-be witches is the possibility of encountering entities from other planes, which may be intent on causing harm or disruption. When one is working solitary there is no one on whom to call for help ... or is there? If you are fortunate enough to find another natural witch to talk to at the start of your studies, they will almost certainly tell you that they never actually feel they are alone. Whatever form you imagine the old gods take, however vague your impression of them may be, there is one thing for certain and that is: *they do exist*. This is something which we should never doubt. They exist and we can communicate with them; not only for our benefit but for theirs, too.

Nowadays it is easy to buy books that give detailed accounts of witchcraft rituals, including those for magical protection. Most, however, involve long and wordy rituals, requiring all manner of tools and accompaniments. Although this information can be useful, it is not practical for natural magic. The point of any ritual is to focus the mind, but this does not mean that a complicated performance is needed.

We humans have become reliant on what we can see and feel on a physical level, and we can turn this reliance to our advantage if we place our trust in the natural world. The next time you go for a walk in the woods, or some remote part of the countryside, just take a few minutes to tune-in to the feel of the place. Ask aloud if the old spirits of the place could offer you a sign to show you that from now on you are going to be in their care.

You can whisper this under your breath, or even mutter it as you walk. It's quite true that witches mutter and it's not without good reason, for we are in regular communication with unseen beings — or at least they remain unseen to most mortals — and quite simply, we enjoy talking to them. So mutter away, even make up a short rhyme if you like, which you can sing quietly to yourself.

An example would be:
> Powers of earth, powers of sea
> have you a gift from thee to me.

This is only a simple, off-the-cuff example; you can no doubt come up with something which feels much better for you. It does, however, serve to display the level of simplicity required and, without making a big thing of it, you have in effect just begun behaving as a natural witch. Now all you have to do is to walk and watch, keep your ears sharp, too, as the old gods often speak to us through the birds and animals. Take note of anything that catches your attention and allow yourself to be drawn towards a particular spot.

Look on the ground and all around you, there will be a 'gift' of some sort waiting for you. This may be a stone, a feather, a stick or some plant — anything, in fact, from the *natural* world. Keep an open mind and do not discard something just because it seems insignificant. In times to come you will learn just how invaluable the most ordinary object can be. After all, this is a direct offering from the gods themselves, which is not something to be taken lightly.

When you do find your gift it will be instantly recognisable. The thrill will be unmistakable and you may well experience a momentary 'oneness with the gods' which is often accompanied by a strange stillness in the air. The birds fall silent, the trees go still, and there is a noticeable 'presence'. This is not a time to be afraid, but rather a time to enjoy the wonder. Pause, wait and absorb the magic.

It hardly needs to be said that some token of thanks should be left for this treasure. Many assume this must be in the form of a coin or crystal but these are not always appropriate. Coins, to me, speak of consumerism, and a crystal left in the earth where it was not formed, may do more harm than good. A much more appropriate way of saying 'thank you' is to look closely at your treasure and decide from which part of the natural kingdom it has come. Think about it for a moment. If it is a feather, then it is obviously the birds who have been sent with your gift; if it is a stone then the earth has offered you one of her bones. After a short contemplation, whisper your thanks before returning home.

Before you go running away with the idea that this was an easy way out .... Leaving a coin, or a crystal, or a lock of your hair, is a polite way of saying: 'ta very much' but unfortunately real witchcraft requires a lot more effort than that. We have a saying up here in the North which is: "You never get owt for nowt" and there is no better example of this than in the realms of magic.

It is a widely recognised anaolgy that somewhere out there on another plane, there is the equivalent of a huge set of weighing scales which constantly fluctuate, weighing up our deeds and assessing our progress. Genuine mistakes and blunders may not alter the balance too drastically, but when we know we should do better, yet still decide to be lazy and cop out, then somehow, at some time, we *will* have to redress the imbalance.

So, considering the importance of our newly acquired gift, it is only fitting that we should make some effort to show our appreciation. This requires another special trip to the place where it was found, only this time we will be taking something appropriate from ourselves to them. In this way we are showing a willingness to make an effort to give, rather than to merely take from the gods. Try to find something suitable to leave behind. If your gift was a feather then it would be thoughtful to take some food for the birds, and if you should happen to know what sort of bird your feather came from, you could research and find the most suitable food to leave. The more effort you put in the more sincere your appreciation will be.

Perhaps we can begin to see how these preliminary preparations for magical protection fit in with the natural world and it will become clearer still when we can feel traces of what our ancestors understood, even if we have to chip away at the veneer of our 21st century concepts and attitudes.

One thing worth bearing in mind at this point is to remember the virtue of patience when dealing with gods and nature spirits. They can all be capricious at times and it is perfectly possible that on our first attempts we may not have found what we felt was a true gift. This is perfectly normal and should not be viewed in any sense as a failure either on their part or ours.

If things take a bit of time to materialise, look upon this as an indication of just how important they are. Something very special could be in the offing, so do not feel disappointed. When things take time they are often highly significant and the full implications may not become apparent for years. When the message does dawn, it will be nothing short of a revelation and well worth the wait.

Let us suppose, however, that we now have our 'gift' or amulet, as this kind of charm is often called. The next step is to sit quietly and consider all that it could represent for us. This does not mean endless researching through books to find out facts, figures and correspondences related to the object, just *think* about what it is, where it came from, when we saw it, how our attention was drawn to etc ...

As an example: let us suppose that we were walking through open fields, or the park, on a Monday during the Wolf Moon. It was cold and windy, and dusk was falling. We had almost given up hope of finding anything when a chattering bird flies into the hedge beside us. Remembering about the ways the old gods speak through the creatures, we stop and watch.

It is a blackbird and when we look closely we can see that it is actually a rich brown colour — a female. For a split second she catches our eye, then with a loud *chit chit chit* she flies out of sight; she calls once more from the gathering darkness, before the light fades completely and everything suddenly goes very quiet. The wind drops and it suddenly feels almost warm, the air is still and heavy.

Moving closer towards the hedge we scour the grass and bare twigs when suddenly a movement catches our eye. There, caught up on a hawthorn is a beautiful wing feather. Carefully lifting it down we can just make out that it is brown and that it still feels warm in our fingers. We know this is for us, and we tuck it safely away in our inside pocket until we arrive home.

Now, what exactly would a natural witch make of all this? The most sensible thing to do is to have a pen and a sheet of paper handy (or better still our magical notebook), and simply jot down everything that we can remember about the encounter. When this list is complete, reflect again about what those things could mean.

Back to our example:

Firstly, the time was dusk, a very magical time when the sun's power is receding to make way for the moon's light. The day was a Monday, the day of the moon, so obviously lunar power is going to play a strong role in our particular magic. Perhaps we will find that women's health and/or magic is going to be something we become especially sensitive towards, and perhaps this is going to be helped by a deepening psychic ability.

The wind which had been playful was suddenly stilled, just as we are active by day and resting at night. Perhaps interpreting dreams will become one of our skills, yet another thing attributed to the tides of the moon. The bird which came close and cast her wing feather was a blackbird — yet she was brown. Perhaps this is a way of warning not to take the words used by others as gospel. It is an illusion that blackbird hens are black, they are not. They are brown because in summer when they tend to the young they are more difficult to see among the browns and greens of the hedgerow.

Nature creates her this way in order to cast an illusion, or in the words of witches 'a glamour', and again this could mean that we should think about illusions and glamours. Are *we* all we appear to be, or are we casting a glamour, too? Is this a trait which we may in some way turn to our advantage? Also the blackbird is brown in order to protect herself and her young. A sure reassurance that the amulet has been sent as a protective charm.

If the above was an accurate account for someone, then the most thoughtful way to offer a 'thank you' would obviously be to return to that same spot and leave some suitable food for a blackbird.

From now on, we must keep in mind that blackbirds are birds to take special notice of, when out walking or going about our daily business: keep eyes and ears tuned in, because some day the messages could be vital. Always remember that the intention of this first tentative step into natural witchcraft was to find an amulet of *protection* so, if you hear an insistent call, don't ever be tempted to ignore it simply because you have something pressing to do.

This message was hammered home to me many years ago, when we were shivering through the depths of a particularly cold and snowy January. We had an engagement to visit some friends for lunch and I knew that our hostess would have gone to a great deal of time and effort to produce a wonderful meal. A couple of hours before we were due to leave the snow started falling rapidly, and settling. The sky looked full and by the time we were about to leave there was a good four inch covering on the roads, and it did seem foolish to even try to set off.

Unfortunately, we had cancelled our last date with these same friends a month earlier and felt somewhat obliged to keep to this arrangement, having twice put them to so much trouble. As we left, one of our resident magpies, sat on the roof chattering furiously, clearly trying to tell us not to be silly. It was still snowing and there sat this magpie, desperately trying to get her message through to us when she could have been tucked up in a nice warm nest.

I paused, I spoke to her, I hesitated. Decisions, decisions. Here we were being told quite plainly not to go, yet in my head I am worrying about social blunders and upsetting people. In disgust the magpie swooped into her bed; she had read my heart and seen that I was intent on ignoring her warning. Feeling a bit sheepish I hurried to the car, muttering my apologies over my shoulder.

Suffice to say, we got two miles out of the village onto a twisty narrow road, and on a particularly sharp left-hander the chap in front lost control and hit a lamppost. To avoid what was left of his car, ours plummeted down into a ditch and, as you can imagine, we never did get our lunch. Fortunately, no one was injured but it cost us dear to replace the car, and all because I didn't listen.

Now, when there is a message for me, I take notice and get my priorities right. We had a narrow escape but it certainly served its purpose in illustrating that there are no half measures on the old path. If you truly choose to walk with the old gods, then you must accept that your dedication will be tested; false promises and half hearted attempts will be scorned. The Old Ones don't suffer fools gladly.

If you are already having doubts about all this, then I suggest that you sit quietly and have a jolly good think. Know thyself is a magical maxim, in fact it is the very first part: To Know, To Dare, To Will and to Keep Silent. Some people are inclined to presume that 'to know' means that we should strive to accumulate knowledge in the academic sense, but the real meaning behind it goes far deeper. Before we can learn anything else of any value, we must know ourselves.

We all have our different strengths and weaknesses, that is what makes us all unique. Using our strengths sensibly is how a true witch develops his or her *own* power. We do *not* scrounge our powers from the gods by performing complicated rituals under the moon, but we do strive to be guided by them. There will be little or no reward for laziness, but there are ample rewards for effort.

Now ... sit quietly with your amulet and reflect on this. What you are in fact doing is meditating but that is an imported word from distant lands, and not one I normally choose to use.

Having got this far, let's look at practical and natural ways in which we can use our amulet. If it happens that our gift was something easy to carry about then this is precisely what we do. Some things are not quite so suitable; for example, the feather mentioned earlier. It may be quite impractical to carry something like this around with us, so we need to take a look at the problem from a different perspective. The true magic lies as much in the *essence* of the amulet as it does in the thing itself, therefore we should think about creating something which carries this essence. This is not half as difficult as it sounds, and with a bit of thought it should be easy enough to create a beautiful and powerful amulet which can travel with us constantly.

Presuming that we are sticking with our original feather - which we have admitted isn't a very practical thing to carry without ruining it - let's examine the possibilities of drawing on its magical essence. To me, a feather speaks of messages, the written word and the power of symbols drawn with quills and ink. Therefore it would be easy enough to transfer the magic of the amulet onto a small disc of paper, it could be an idea to consider using an ink *called* 'doves blood' (no doves have been killed to make it!) to retain a mental link to birds for this purpose and to remember the lunar connections, too.

Refer back to the original list of associations and let the imagination run free. Consider the tides of the moon, work at an appropriate one, work by candlelight simply because it's so much more evocative, and simply draw the magic of the experience onto the paper. By all means use symbols or squiggles which only you can understand, this is *your* magic and yours alone.

When satisfied with the end result and you feel your concentration beginning to wane, lay the feather across the paper and leave it overnight on a windowsill that catches the moonlight. During the day tuck it away secretly before placing it under the moon again at night. Do this until the eve of the next full moon when you can wrap up your feather and place it somewhere safe and secret. Your amulet is now ready to use. You may like to keep it in a little hand stitched pouch, so you can either wear it or carry it in your pocket, briefcase or handbag.

Some may have noticed that there has been no mention so far about cleansing or consecrating the amulet, and this is with good reason. Anything which comes directly to us from nature is already consecrated, and to do anything else would be to effectively strip it of all its magical properties, leaving a totally useless object that would be incapable of generating any powers of protection — or anything else either.

All this activity will have taken us well through the Wolf Moon but before we look forward to the next, take note of the dark tide at the end of the Wolf Moon. This is a good time to reflect upon everything that we have done and thought about. Before the tide turns we need to take out our notebook and write up all that we have discovered. Be vigilant in trying to remember small details; how you felt, what the weather was like, wildlife you've encountered, etc. It is amazing how quickly we forget things which can prove to be of vital importance at a later date.

In years to come you will get a great deal of pleasure looking back over these notes and perhaps someday they may even be passed on to another generation. Treasure them, keep them safe and secret — they are gems of the Mother whom you are slowly coming to know.

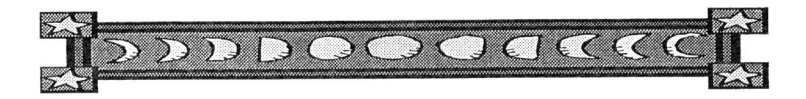

THE EARTH TIDE
February—The Storm Moon

The Storm Moon is so-called for the unpredictable and changeable weather in February. It is a month of contradictions; on one hand we see the first tentative signs of spring emerging, yet on the other we can still fall prey to heavy snowfalls and even thunder storms. One day may be surprisingly mild and bright sunshine, while the following may find us practically house-bound due to deep snow drifts. Out in the fields and gardens we see early buds and even tiny flowers, braving the cold to emerge into the weak sunshine; Nature urging them to draw life from the light and warmth, yet all the time risking death at the hands of a cruel frost.

Though this is a time of cold, biting winds we know we are moving towards the return of warmth and sunshine. The first stirrings of new life are all around and bulbs that have been sleeping through the winter, are now pushing through as the sun gently warms the earth again.

We are slowly entering the elemental tide of Earth.

With this moon we can identify our first tentative steps into the realms of magic. We accept that although some deep, subconscious urge tells us that this is the path we must follow, at the same time we must also realise there is a vast reservoir of knowledge from which we have not even drawn, and that it may take several lifetimes before we truly come to understanding.

Here we stand, like the first flowers in the fields, with the vast and confusing universe stretching out before us. The future is uncertain but with the gods of nature to accompany us, we should try to view this as an adventure that although challenging, can offer a rich spiritual goal. We can and we *will* weather the storms ahead.

Traditionally the Storm Moon is also a time for purification.

On the physical level it is a time to start spring cleaning. Just as the badger will clean out his sett and the vixen will clean out her earth, carrying fresh bedding in preparation for the new season's offspring. This tells us that at this beginning of the Earth Tide, we should effectively be looking at ourselves and our homes.

The witch's home is a magical place and, as witches appear especially skilled at accumulating clutter, it is a good time to kick up a storm of our own and have a good sort out. This may not seem like a very magical thing to do, but it is important to remember that *all* forms of magic need to have an outlet on the physical plane in order for it to work – in other words, it requires 'earthing'. It is not a good idea to drift into the realms of fantasy and visualisation all the time, since this is a fast route to going round the bend, to put it bluntly. Far from enhancing anyone's magic it will be more likely to dispel it altogether.

Getting to grips with some mundane task like taking the curtains down and disturbing a few spiders will successfully balance the magic done during the Wolf Moon and will serve to ground (or 'earth') the magic which has already started to flow through our lives.

As we go through our home like the proverbial white tornado, try to imagine that we are also dispelling all the old arguments, old prejudices and in fact anything which has not been beneficial in the past. See and feel the freshness and the brightness of your newly cleaned rooms/space, get into every cupboard on both the mundane and psychic levels, if you can. The more effort we put in, the greater the reward will be, until eventually we can stand back and know that our 'space' in this life is as clean as we can get it.

Towards the end of the Storm Moon – having completed all this hard work on the physical level, it is time to turn again to magical working. One of the reasons why it is important to watch the unfolding of the universal cycles is so that magical operations can be timed to coincide with a favourable tide. This is one of the ways in which we put into practice the saying 'living in harmony' with the world; knowing how to harness these natural tides to our advantage and increase our witch-power.

Because a rite of purification is intended to help us disperse all those negative aspects of ourselves which we feel have an adverse influence on our well-being, it is suited to the magic of a waning moon. Some writers in the past have mistakenly implied that the dark tide of the moon (the three nights before the new moon), is a time of destruction, evil deeds and sorcery. *This is absolute rubbish.* The dark of the moon is certainly more mysterious and there is a very special kind of magic attuned to it, but this is no reason to avoid it, or be afraid of it.

Within certain levels of magic a witch may choose to work at this time with 'dark*ish* deeds' in mind — because all magic, whatever its aims, comes in 'forty shades of grey'. Rest assured, a witch intent on causing harm via a magical application will not be confined by any lunar tide; a witch intent on causing harm is likely to remain undaunted by pretty much *anything!*

There is a trend among the pagan community to portray witchcraft as being somehow goody-goody in order to dispel some of the more dreadful myths that have surrounded it. It is easy to understand where these ideas are coming from, and the intention behind such publicity is no doubt of the best, but it is just as misleading to try to portray all witches as being young, selfless, well intentioned and almost saintly, as it was to portray us all as being evil old crones.

The honest among us do not pretend to be perfect, but the wise among us do at least *try* to use our powers with the best intentions for all concerned. There is no such thing as black or white magic; magical energy itself is neutral just like electricity. It's *how* the individual puts it to use that defines whether it is beneficial or dangerous. This does not mean, however, that we can never be angry or unpleasant, since even the most placid of people can resort to 'dark deeds' if pushed far enough.

In the unlikely event that someone should be pushed to those extremes, it is up to *them* as an individual to balance those scales, and most witches prefer not to have to resort to such dealings. The aftermath of casting a spell to bring about the downfall of another has such devastating results on the sender that this is usually reason enough for most of us to find a more reasonable way of dealing with the problem. We cannot and should not use our magical abilities to simply get our own way over everything in life, as with the macrocosm there must always be a balance. In other words, we have to learn to take the rough with the smooth and not take our spite out on other people — even if we think they deserve it.

If witchcraft was a means to an end, wherein all led a charmed life, then it is extremely doubtful whether christianity would ever have got a foot in the door. At the same time the life of a witch *is* charmed in many ways, and most of us would not change who we are for all the world. Indeed, it is not even up to us to consider such a thing. There is a saying that witches are born and not made — and there is some truth in this. If it is our destiny to walk the old paths with the old gods then nothing in this world (or any other) is going to stop us.

So before we embark on this path it makes sense to ensure that we are as well prepared as possible. While chatting with a friend one day about preparations for magic she revealed that she always wore fishnet stockings, basque and suspenders beneath her robe. As she put it: "Well if you're going to meet the Horned God you want to look your best".... although this isn't quite what we mean by presenting ourselves as well as possible, I *did* know what she meant.

With that particular witch-friend in mind let's get back to the subject of magical preparations which does go some way towards explaining the witches' attitude to the gods.

On the physical level most of us feel that as we are going to be in the presence of our gods, it is only fitting that we should make some effort to make ourselves presentable, much the same as anyone would if they were going to be meeting anyone of importance. Sadly this is an area which is overlooked by some 'modern' pagans who prefer the unkempt look.

It may surprise some to learn that during the dreadful 'burning times' one of the things which aroused suspicion of witchcraft was when a person had been singled out for being *too clean*. There is an old saying among us 'as above so below' and the idea of being physically clean equates to the idea of being spiritually clean—which brings us back to our cleansing ritual.

Remember that as magic must have some way of manifesting on the physical level, so it is with magical purification. It would be a total waste of time to expect a rite of purification to work if the body we give it to work through (which is after all *our* temple) is dirty. In this light it is not a bad idea to consider how well our lifestyle and eating habits compliment our temple. Whilst I certainly wouldn't want to steer anybody onto any unwholesome diet of total abstinence from the good things in life, it is a good idea to strive for a healthy, happy body from which to work.

When the moon is waning to dark and the time is right for your rite of purification, lock the door, unplug the phone and run a good hot bath. Add to this a good handful of sea salt and, if you have any knowledge of herbs (or a suitable book to help you), a sachet of appropriate herbs to hang under the hot tap. As this is part of a magical rite, enhance the special importance of the night by having candles in the bathroom, purifying sandalwood burning (in joss or cones) and even some relaxing music playing in the background.

Lay back in the hot water, think about who *you think you are*, and any ways in which you would like to improve yourself. What positive things can you do, what negative traits could you honestly do to lose? Mull these things over from every angle until you are absolutely certain about the aspects of your 'old self' you would like to discard. Once you have these things firmly fixed in your mind, get out and dress in something clean, loose and comfortable before picking up your amulet and going to sit quietly in the darkness.

Now take up a pen (if your amulet was a feather this could have become a quill pen suitable for magical use) and write down on a clean piece of paper all the qualities you wish to discard. The list can be as long or short as it needs to be. When it is complete, look at it again and when you are certain of it, light a white candle and gaze into the flame. Fire magic is especially potent at the time of the Storm Moon because this is springtime when the sun warms the Earth back to life. The waking Earth Goddess is in power and it is to her you are making your supplication. When you feel ready, either holding your treasured amulet or wearing it as the case may be, it is time to ask the goddess to listen.

If you can create your own words of power then so much the better but just to give you an idea I suggest the following be used as a guideline or inspiration.

"Gracious powers of the holy tides, I humbly beseech thee to hear these words spoken from the heart. My spirit yearns to walk with you in the old paths of magic and my soul strives to serve you. Take from me that which is not required by thee, and leave me pure in heart and mind, that I may be a fit and proper servant."

Wait in silence for a few minutes, gazing into the candle flame. At some point you may well get a strong impression of a presence surrounding you; at the least the atmosphere will feel calm and as this is your sacred space, you can relax and let all your negativity be washed away. When you sense that the time is right, using a small pair of tongs, touch the list you made to the candle flame and watch as the paper burns to ashes. Carry the ash to the door and cast it away to the winds before leaving a small offering outside for the wildlife.

If it's at all practical, try to go straight to bed after this ritual without speaking to anyone as there is a strong possibility that you may have a prophetic dream. If this does happen, make detailed notes about it as soon as you wake because at some point the message it conveys will be highly significant to you.

In the days and weeks to come it is important to allow the magic of the Storm Moon to manifest in your everyday life. Be prepared for some turbulence as you make these adjustments, friends and family will also have to adjust to the new, more positive you, so be patient. Even though *you* may understand the reason for these differences others may not, so take things gradually and weather the storm with as much dignity as you can muster: patience will surely pay off.

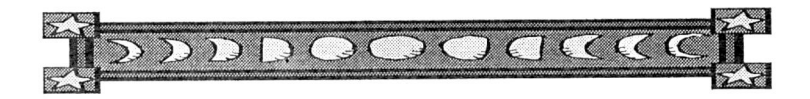

THE EARTH TIDE
March—The Chaste Moon

The Chaste Moon reflects the purity of the new spring. There is definitely more activity now; the energy of new life is growing daily. Out in the fields and in the garden there is much more evidence of spring. Even though it is still cold and the snow has not quite relinquished its grip; the primeval urge of nature is growing stronger, shoots emerge from their winter hiding places. Just like a child in the womb, nature is kicking and thriving, increasing in vigour with each passing day.

The sun's power is increasing too, and let's not forget that this in turn increases the 'power' of the moon. After all, the light we see shining from the moon comes originally from the sun, so it stands to reason that we should *all* feel the stirring of spring. It is not merely a joke to say that this is the time when a young man's fancy turns to love (or more appropriately sex) ... the poor chap can't help it! Animals, birds, fish, plants and humans will all succumb to the desires of the old primeval force of nature.

Under the circumstances, at first glance the name 'Chaste Moon' may not seem very appropriate, considering the amount of sexual activity going on — but it is the *innocence* of this energy that counts. Everything is new, young and in its virgin form, even the more mature among us, whether this is mankind, trees or animals. The physical body may be mature but the rejuvenating Earth Tides are fresh and vibrant. These are brand new days dawning and they naturally contain brand new spring energy.

This is what the Chaste Moon signifies on the subtle levels of magic. Not everything is obvious in nature and we have to learn to be more receptive to those things which appear veiled in secrecy. Think of a huge old tree which may have stood for sixty years or more. The buds it sprouts in early spring are still as tiny and fragile as the ones it produced as a mere sapling, but they are each and every one still *new* buds. So it is with magical development. If ever there is a time of year when the circle of the year is most poignantly displayed then it is now.

What better inspiration to natural understanding than the age-old cycles of birth, death and rebirth as a reminder of the eternal re-emergence of life.. What better time could there be to begin to cast the witches' circle.

To many this will conjure up images of robes and candles, thuribles and chalices. Under different circumstances all this regalia can be very meaningful and greatly enhance the occasion but in *natural* witchcraft all these trappings are viewed as being decorative rather than essential. The only essential bit of equipment—other than ourselves — is our amulet. Many of us do carry a small knife for *purely practical reasons*, but we will come to that later.

The circle of protection is simple yet it is 100% effective. Our amulet (or charm) already gives us protection from the gods themselves and all that needs to be done is to sit quietly in a place where we won't be disturbed, so that we can concentrate. If you can make the effort to return to the exact spot where you found your amulet, then so much the better. For this is a particular place where the natural gods will recognise you immediately and so the links will be much stronger. In fact, it is a good idea to make a note in your journal to return to this special place every year on the anniversary of this day in order to say a special 'thank you'. And to boost the power of the amulet.

Holding our amulet in our hands, we close our eyes and relax. Focussing on all that it means to us; all the associations that it represents as we feel the energy pulsating gently. Now in our mind's eye we begin to 'see' a bluish light tinged with green, streaming from the amulet. It has a faintly phosphorous glow and the colours remind us of the blues that can sometimes be seen in a lightning flash. This aura is not merely a figment of our imagination. It has long been recognised (even by the most bigoted of scientists), that this is the force of nature.

Once we are comfortable with this stream of energy, we try to push and mould it with our mind. Projecting it out in front of ourselves, stretching out into infinity; drawing it back and have it swirling in spirals and, finally, forming it into a ball of blue light which has a tail like a comet trailing behind it. Projecting this ball out to within three feet of ourselves before making it circle around us, leaving a trail of glowing fire. We swoop the ball over our head, underneath us through the earth and out again until we have a glowing sphere that envelopes us completely.

This is *your* circle of protection and *only* those influences which offer their services to protect *you* can enter. All these natural energies or influences combine to make up the protective circle, requiring no salt, water, candles or incense; no quarter guardians. In this sacred space *your* auras are as one, mingling totally and freely, joining forces to create a sphere in which preservation and protection are paramount.

Here we can sit a while and enjoy the feeling of being as one within the charmed circle, and all that it embodies, before allowing the blue light to be drawn gently back into the amulet. We must practice this exercise until we can enlarge our circle at will. Very soon we will be able to do it in the twinkling of an eye.

If at any time in the future, someone or something intent on harm should attempt to come into *your* 'space', the spirit within your charm will leap to your defence and create a barrier, even though you may not have been aware that you were in any danger.

This kind of protection, however, does not come without some form of bargain or 'pact'. Remember the old Yorkshire saying about "owt for nowt", well, this also certainly applies in magic. For as long as we expect our charms to work for us, it requires us to remember to appreciate it. For our example, this could mean remembering daily to feed the blackbirds. If all this seems like too much hard work, then forget the idea of being a witch.

Hopefully, those reading this book will be made of sterner stuff, and the effort required will seem a small enough price to pay when there are such ample rewards to be gained. If these first three moons have been worked through with sincerity then you will no doubt already feel a difference inside yourself. This early work is probably the hardest part and certainly sorts the "men from the boys" but it does give a thorough grounding to any witch trying to find the path. As the adventures get more challenging and exciting, it will be the ones with the firmest foundations who come through best.

It is also vital that we have an absolute unshakeable faith in our magic. Our charm of protection needs us to maintain faith in it in order for it to function at its best, so just because we start to do other interesting things in the following moons, we should not be tempted to forget to show our appreciation to those who provided it. Make a point to feed the birds each day. If we make every effort to feed them at roughly the same time each day come hail or shine, what we are in fact doing is performing a simple ritual.

So in these first three months you have learned to create a charm, mutter a charm, do a magical cleansing, cast a circle of protection *and* perform a ritual. Not bad going for starters, and there is plenty left still to learn.

Though what we have touched on so far may *appear* to be easy, anyone truly working through these things would already admit that there is more in them than meets the eye. By now there should be a subtle but distinct transformation going on in the 'inner temple' and this will be noticed by the old gods. Family and friends may well be seeing a difference in you, too, but do not be tempted to reveal your new-found talents. Remain mysterious, smile enigmatically but tell them nothing, for in ways like this we emulate our gods.

This is yet another example of casting a glamour, because what is hidden or barely revealed is always far more tantalising than that which is made immediately obvious. Casting this type of a glamour is not the same as being deceptive, for a deliberate deception implies dishonesty which is not a trait to be embraced. There is a fine line between the two which is often difficult to define but the differences are easy to sense inwardly. Witchcraft is often called the Craft of the Wise, and a person who indulges in deliberately misleading others is sometimes referred to as being crafty. It is a fine line to walk and one which can only be understood by experience; let your conscience be your guide on this one.

For instance, I can recall a situation years ago when I had been invited to the home of an acquaintance to meet a handful of people who were interested in the Old Ways, but who had no previous experience of working with them. Our host had requested that I talk with them and maybe give a few hints on how best to follow their individual interests.

I was not keen to go but in the end I decided to accept because it seemed churlish to reject the opportunity to meet and talk with people who were in all probability perfectly nice and genuine. By the end of a week I had convinced myself that it was the right thing to do, since there is no harm in talking to people who are drawn to the old gods. They obviously wished to exchange ideas and feelings with someone who had a bit more experience. At the end of the day none of us know everything and, at times, we *can* learn from one another. It can be enjoyable to relax in the company of like-minded souls, where we can talk more freely amongst ourselves, even discover those who walk a path alongside our own, exchanging our discoveries as we go.

So on the appointed evening I got into my best bib and tucker, and with a feeling of pleasant anticipation, set off. After the initial introductions, the talk soon turned to things of a more magical nature with everyone happily chipping in with their thoughts and impressions. Up to this point I felt it was sensible to keep in the background and listen to what the others had to say before committing myself in conversation. Instinct, or a private message of protection, made me hold back from disclosing anything about the way I work, or the things I do, and by the end of the evening I was convinced that this *had* been the right reaction.

It soon became all too apparent that what these people were really hoping to do was to pick *my* brains. In a way it was reminiscent of the burning times: it was nothing short of an Inquisition. As the wine and conversation flowed everyone appeared to be vying for approval from everyone else. The old egos came shooting out from behind the glamour of innocence, and pretty soon it was a verbal game of 'king of the castle' which, incidentally is a game which has its roots way back in antiquity and is actually well worth studying. On this particular occasion, however, it was wholly unsuited to what was supposed to be an evening of exchange not competition.

There were those present who had come along under the guise of 'beginner on the threshold of discovery', when in fact they obviously had a little knowledge and wanted more. They perhaps thought that if they showed off about the bits they *did* know, that anyone with any genuine ability would be silly enough to talk freely with them and reveal things which had hitherto eluded them. More wine flowed and the conversations got sillier and sillier, with people making even wilder claims about all manner of mystical experiences in order to gain credibility — or at least that was the impression.

Eventually someone turned to me and asked me which method I used when I wanted to work with elementals, to which I replied in wide eyed innocence "Oh, I don't dabble in that sort of thing, it's too dangerous." The disappointment was palpable and there is no doubt in my mind that these people probably thought I was desperately boring, not to say a miserable excuse for a witch. Soon after that I made my excuses and left because there was nothing for me among those people.

Perhaps they continued as friends and helped one another along the way and, if this is the case, I wish them well. Sometimes we have to face up to the fact that for the most part it is wiser to keep silent, to remain as a little island, protecting those treasures we hold so dear. Maybe this pure inner island that is our own natural magic is the real Isle of Avalon. This is something that you might like to think about throughout the rest of this moon. Practice casting your circle, and reflect upon the importance of what you are protecting by your silence.

In this way, you are once again learning to give and take, for just as the old gods of nature have offered you *their* protection, so you can repay this by keeping *their* secrets under *your* protection .'As above, so below' and yet another example of how magic must manifest itself on our physical plane.

We have briefly mentioned the knife that all working witches carry. At one time this was with us at all times but due to various changes in the law, this is no longer possible. The original reason for carrying a knife was a purely practical one; whenever we are out and about, there is a chance that we will see some plant that we know could be useful to us. There are also laws governing the picking or removing (whole or in part) of many wild plants, and these must also be taken into consideration. Nowadays, we must accept that carrying a knife (with the exception of a small pocket knife) and removing plants is illegal and so the traditional witches' knife must remain at home.

The magical associations of the knife have become distorted in recent years, with the purely ritual tool being referred to as an athame. In traditional British Old Craft, a knife is a knife, as simple as that. We use it to dig for roots, and to remove twigs and stems; to prepare food and to eat with at our sacred meals; we inscribe candles with it; carve magical symbols and, if needs be, threaten an unwanted entity with it. The witches' knife is not a pretty, flimsy, impractical object to be waved around for no good reason. What the thing looks like is absolutely immaterial, it's what we do with it that counts.

For reasons of continuing tradition and practicality, it is still a good idea to try and obtain a special knife. Ideally, it should have a wooden handle, as this is more natural, but the length and style of the blade is entirely up to the individual using it.

Knives (like swords in ritual magic) conjure up an image of fire and forge. This magic is linked to the old smith-gods, and it is a good idea to think about blessing it through the element of fire when you first make your choice. All the elements are present within a knife, therefore it is appropriate for any kind of magic. The ore is mined from the Earth; the raw materials are fashioned by Fire; the fire needs Air to sustain the fierce heat; while the smith will dip the blade into Water many times before hammering the blade into shape. So it is easy to understand why witches recognise and respect the magical associations of their working knife.

If you do not already have a knife that feels special to you, now may be the time to consider trying to find one. One rule applies in the buying of it — and this dates back a very long way. The price of the knife must never be haggled over, not should you expect to receive any change. You must be prepared to hand over the exact price. If it is received as a gift, a silver coin must be given in exchange.

These first three moons have offered plenty to think about, but now the fires of the gods are burning brighter and the energy of spring is gathering momentum. It's time to revel in the riot of colour which is abundant now and to gaze in wonder at the beauty and splendour of the land as we approach the Spring Equinox. The birds are busy; the hare is dancing wildly in the sheer joy of life and we can begin to look forward to Roodmass (more commonly referred to nowadays as Beltaine) — the Seed Moon, a time to let our hair down.

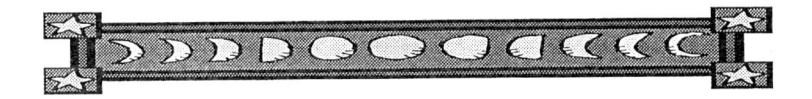

THE EARTH TIDE
April—The Seed Moon

The glorious feast of Roodmass has to be one of the favourite festivals among witches. It is a time of sheer fun and enjoyment, and a time of merriment and courtship but it is difficult to decide whether Roodmass or Hallowmass (called Samhain in modern Craft) has caused the most uproar among the clergy in the past.

Traditional witches have always had a candid approach to both sex and death, and just these aspects of our beliefs alone are enough to incite criticism, malice and in some cases downright hatred. Today's society finds it so much easier to feel free to express their sexual nature, and the old moralities imposed by the church are fast being reassessed (much to their horror). We have returned to a more healthier attitude, and in this atmosphere of relaxed spontaneity we can truly appreciate the essence of Roodmass.

Anyone seeking confirmation of this needs look no further than the fields and gardens. All around, birds and animals are answering to this wonderful natural energy, which is the climax of the earthy spring tide. It's the time to forget the cares and worries of winter; food is becoming plentiful again; and the urge to reproduce becomes paramount.

We only need to watch and listen to the birds in the garden to know that their minds are fixed firmly on one thing and one thing only. There will be frantic nest building and much chasing and swooping as everything plays 'take your partner' for this fabulous natural dance, with the grand finale played out regardless of what- or whoever is around at the time.

Critics of witchcraft would have a field day if it was openly suggested that humans should behave like the animals and birds, and it is hardly practical to risk ending up making a public spectacle of yourself by doing so. There is a time and place for everything and some degree of restraint is only common sense and good manners — but this should not be seen as being moralistic in any way. Actually, there are sound *magical* reasons for exercising restraint at certain times, because it is precisely this restraint that raises the energies, much the same as allowing pressure to build up in a pressure cooker.

This building of energy can be recognised within the changing seasons themselves, from the quiet tide of winter, to the awakening and rising tide in spring, through to the full blooded splendour of summer, till nature finally reaches a climax in autumn with the bursting and showering of the fruits and seeds. So it must be within ourselves. What begins magically with a fleeting thought, develops into an idea, which in turn leads to the drive which motivates us into taking action, and finally culminates in the completion of the act.

There is a considerable amount of misunderstanding over what we, in magical terms, mean by *sexual energy*, since it is presumed to refer to creatures and humans, in particular, indulging in sexual intercourse. Though this is accurate enough on a mundane level, it is only a small part of the picture. Because *all* energy can be viewed as being sexual in that it is the movement caused by two opposing forces coming into contact with each other which creates the energy. The two universal forces of nature, one positive, the other negative (or receptive), working together to create the life-force, which in turn creates the wonderful world of nature that sustains us all. When we begin to think about harnessing ourselves to this great universal power, we begin to understand the *true* source of a witch's power. By the simple knowledge that we are part of this vast continuous flow of natural energy, we realise just how privileged we are. Not only are we part of it, but we have the intellect to understand it, and therefore appreciate it too.

The Seed Moon more or less speaks for itself. The gathering power of the Earth Tide has reached its peak and the earth is once again rich and fertile. The seeds which were showered down in the orgasm of autumn, and which have lain dormant through the cold, can now safely start to sprout. The pregnancy of summer is about to begin, but first the cyclical marriage must be consummated.

Above all else, Roodmass is a time of celebration. We have made it safely through the winter; we have watched the spring tide gather strength. The trees are greening, the new shoots are growing daily and all around us, creatures are pairing off and going all out on the fertility bit. We have felt our own sap rising and felt the animal urges coming to the fore.

One word of caution regarding all this wonderful energy buzzing about: this is not to be taken as an excuse to throw the nearest fanciable person over the meat counter in Sainsbury's. A little discretion doesn't go amiss regarding who, when and where — and if you have a partner who is comfortable about joining in with your celebrations, there is absolutely no reason why a bit of what you fancy cannot be included. If the weather is good, then celebrate outdoors. Just pick your place carefully and try to avoid the local gamekeeper. *Coitus interuptus* is no fun, and especially when faced with a large pair of wellies and a double-barrelled shotgun. Again ... use your discretion and a measure of common sense.

One of the loveliest things which should be flourishing at this time (weather permitting) is the hawthorn (may or hagthorn). The delicate creamy-white flowers are sacred to the goddess of spring herself and even though it is not advisable to have the blossoms and boughs in the house after midnight, they do make beautiful decorations for a day. The hawthorn is a faery tree, and the particular 'spirits' or elementals who inhabit the may are well-known for having great fun at the expense of us mortals, given half a chance. To be on the safe side, take the blossoms and boughs out of the house before the moon comes up - that way the Faere Folk will not be drawn to coming in!

Another custom linked to Roodmass is that of getting up as dawn is breaking, to bathe in the dew — a custom reputed to bestow beauty upon any maiden who can slip out unnoticed as the birds are rising, and bath her face with the chilly Roodmass dew. I sneak out to enjoy this bit of fun myself and, if I am certain that no one is peaking over the hedge, I freely admit to going the whole hog and stripping off my frillies to roll in it. It's an extremely invigorating experience and one I thoroughly recommend. Though as to its effectiveness it is not for me to say, since my status is nearer crone than maiden!

If the day of the full moon doesn't happen to fall at the weekend, then do consider actually booking a day off work. This way we can enjoy both the day and the evening, making it really special. If you have a willing partner who can do the same, then the two of you can really push the boat out, making it truly a time to remember. It is worth making every effort because this is how the old magic of the seasons become fixed firmly in our minds.

On the morning of the full Seed Moon, slip quietly away to your garden, or the fields, and take a few moments to greet the day. There may still be elementals around at this time when the world is quiet, so tread stealthily so that you don't alarm them. To some people this might all sound very fanciful, but I can assure you that, from experience, I know this to be the case. I will never forget, slipping away silently from the cottage, and down into the garden long before anyone else was about.

As I often do, I had taken a drop of milk and a biscuit to leave under the hedge as an offering of friendship. To my surprise, an 'elemental' was sitting in the early morning sun, right in the roots of the old hawthorn hedge. As I bent forward, the poor creature let out a squeak and leapt into the hedge, while I let out a squeak and leaped backwards. I don't know which of us was the more surprised to see the other, but ever since I have regularly left a special treat at the same spot, and have been fortunate enough to see he, she or it, on several occasions.

This nature sprite is still shy and nervous but I speak quietly and go about whatever I'm doing with consideration. They are sensitive little things and any relationship with us humans can be very risky for them. Given encouragement, however, some of them can soon become bold but if you should ever get one trapped inside the house, they can cause untold mischief. Nature spirits are best left outside where they feel free and to encourage them inside is asking for trouble.

Happenings such as this are no doubt where the tales of Roodmass, and the lore regarding the hawthorn, spring from. In early times, when Britain was the land of the *real* Faere Folk, everyone one would probably have had an experience similar to my own, and no doubt there were plenty of tales told about the mischief and tricks played upon the unsuspecting, if our folk-lore is anything to go by.

On the special festival of Roodmass, try to retrieve some of this old magic and begin the day by bathing your face in the morning dew. In this way you are making yourself radiant, ready to weave your enchantments of love on your heart's desire. Lift your face to the sun and let his warming rays dry your skin naturally, smile, sing, even dance barefoot if that's how it makes you feel. Leave your cares behind, wash the winter blues away, and above all let your spirit soar to embrace the coming of summer.

This response of pure joy could be your gift to nature, a way of harmonising with the joy of the earth at the return of warmth and abundance. It should be a release of energy and yet it should enliven you and leave you full of vitality, ready to enjoy what lies ahead. Before you return to your home, take a few sprigs of hawthorn to decorate the doorway. Always try to respect the trees, take the cuttings swiftly and with as little dragging and shaking of boughs as you can. Contrary to popular belief it is kinder to cut swiftly and cleanly with a sharp pair of secateurs, than it is to struggle with a blunt decorative knife. Whisper your thanks, and before the day is out, leave a little something for the nature spirits: your consideration will be appreciated.

Food and drink have always played a large part in any celebrations and Roodmass is no exception. Now is the time to put together a special feast, and this, too, is a way of continuing the traditions of a very old custom. Originally there would have been a hunt, where the men could get their blood running as they hunted the stags on this day. The victorious man who killed their quarry would have been presented with the antlers, which he would have worn with great pride. This man would have had his pick of the most beautiful maidens whom he would woo throughout the day.

The huge need-fire would have cooked the meat for the feast and, when night falls, and the moon sailed overhead, there would have been much feasting and drinking. The whole thing would have culminated in the Stag King taking the Maiden as his own, and if the magic was good, this would result in the birth of a child. These children were respected as being special, and would have been trained in the magical arts, so that the magic of nature could be passed down the generations.

As well as the King and his Lady celebrating the great marriage, everyone else would no doubt get caught up in the magic, and many a ' greenwood marriage' was consummated on Roodmass night. Children from these unions would be born in the early spring the following year. Try to remember the old essence of Roodmass as you celebrate, for even though our modern festivities are pale by comparison, we can still capture the spirit of the day if we try.

When planning a Roodmass feast, try to think in terms of natural food, and dishes which can be eaten easily without the need for a lot of cutlery. Try if you can to get organic produce, and at all costs avoid things which come in lurid cellophane wrappers and riddled with colouring and preservatives. There is nothing traditional about rubbish like this, and it is hardly sharing with, and partaking of, nature's gifts when you know full well that it was commercially produced in a factory and probably handled by those with no affinity with nature. Keep things simple, fresh and wholesome—and visit a farmer's market if you don't grow the produce yourself.

A very simple but enjoyable Roodmass feast could be:

One large wholemeal loaf (home made if possible)
A dozen chicken drumsticks roasted and cooled.
Some hard boiled eggs.
Home made apple pie with fresh cream
Several bottles of speciality ale
or a couple of bottles of decent wine.

Nowadays nearly all wines contain artificial ingredients, so if you can't get homemade wine anywhere, then ale is a better choice.

There is now a brewery who specialises in ales and beers made to authentic recipes and many are named appropriately especially for our celebrations. These are delicious and I cannot recommend them highly enough; they are not expensive and to our delight they are now widely available in most supermarkets. Even the labels are evocative and they make a fine accompaniment to any feast, and any self respecting witch should always have an odd one or two stashed away, just in case ...

Years ago we would have been pretty certain of a fine sunny day, which was perfect for our outdoor celebrations, but it's not always a certainty these days. With a bit of luck the day will be fair enough to pack up your feast and head for the hills. If, however, it happens to be throwing it down, then an indoor feast will have to suffice. It's nice to bring some fresh flowers in, and if there isn't enough growing in your garden, then a few shop-bought ones will still mark the day as being special.

For fun I always wind coloured ribbons round my clothes prop as a makeshift maypole, and far from upsetting my neighbours, I have had several requests to join in! One lady brings her grandchildren who dance and wind with peals of laughter, and even though they don't grasp the full significance of what they are doing, we are all working the old magic just the same. With my old peg basket as a percussion instrument we make our music up as we go along and with some shared apples and a jug of ale we've had some rare fun.

The emphasis on this festival is one of *innocent fun.* This is because the Seed Moon follows the Chaste Moon, hence the hint that though the time is lusty, it still respects the young and innocent. Try to keep this sentiment through the day. By all means let any children of family and friends join in with the feasting if you like. Though if you do, remember to provide soft fruity drinks for them in place of the wine or ale. Any adult activity can be saved until the children are tucked up in bed, and after a day running about outdoors, they should sleep like logs. In some ways a day like this, with the hidden promise of a romantic night kept under wraps, is another way of learning to exercise the ability to save up magical energy until the time is right to release it.

If on the other hand you celebrate Roodmass in a solitary fashion, there is no reason to find any less enjoyment in it. You can still arrange to have a day off work so that you can plan a whole day doing as you please. Getting up early, you can still slip outside and bath in the fresh dew, and there is nothing to stop you making up a small feast which you can enjoy outdoors - weather permitting.

It is often the case that at times like this, when the old magic is closer to the surface, that those celebrating a solitary rite can have beautiful and enlightening experiences which are deeply personal and reassuring. I would go so far as to say that these stunning revelations usually *only* happen when one is alone.

If you are going to celebrate on your own then it is entirely up to you how you do it. The preceding paragraphs will have given you the feeling of the day and with a little imagination it can still be a very special time but remember that Roodmass is part of the natural tide and not a fixed date on a calendar.

The evening of Roodmass is a wonderful time to hold a bonfire if you can, whether this is in a corner of your garden, or in some local woods. The option of our own garden is often safer, which is a shame, but I do not want to put forward suggestions which may result in anyone putting themselves in any potentially dangerous situation.

As I said earlier, magic needs to ground itself on an earthly level, and our protective charms are no exception. Excellent though they are, it is nothing short of foolhardy to go wandering the woods at night alone. It is nothing magical which poses any threat, it is the possibility of encountering other humans who may be up to no good. Use common sense at all times.

If you do choose to light the need-fire, then in token of the old ways, you should extinguish all forms of lighting and heating in your home first. This is symbolic of a new fire, a new season with new energy. If you wish to make it *very* traditional you could try to find small branches of the seven sacred woods with which to light it, but for natural magic this isn't strictly necessary. However, one word of warning, do not *ever* burn elder wood on a domestic or need-fire: you have been warned!

For couples celebrating round the need-fire, I don't think you need me to spell anything out . . . the magic of the full moon, the flickering flames, the fire sprites dancing, the heavy scent of the hawthorn so like the smell of a woman, the last dregs of the ale or wine ... you get the message—and enjoy!

Likewise if you are alone, absorb the energies, enjoy the night, and share the atmosphere, you will know instinctively what feels right for you.

Around about now, you might like to consider starting to collect some working tools, and even possibly a robe of some sort. This being the Seed Moon, it is an appropriate time to plant these ideas into your mind. Don't forget that any self-respecting witch is going to want to harvest herbs later in the year, as well as gathering all manner of interesting plants and ingredients that can go towards blending incenses. Though the burning of incenses may sound more like ritual magic, do not forget that many plants and herbs, when correctly prepared, can in fact help to cure certain ailments. Added to that, a nicely prepared incense is a gift to the spirits of air, and there is nothing quite like an outdoor fire with beautiful incense burning on it. Many people agree that nothing shifts their mind into magical mode quite as instantly as the evocative smell of a familiar incense, and I entirely agree with them.

Roodmass has a wonderful atmosphere all its own, and it is fitting that you should strive to enjoy it to the full, but at some point when the ale or wine is flowing, do please take a few moments to sincerely thank the 'Ol' Lad and Lass' for their guidance. Raise a cup or glass to the stars or the sun, and wish them well, and always tip a little onto the earth as a libation.

A nice libation was told to me many years ago by a witch friend, and it goes as follows;

> *"Although I have nothing to give you which is not already yours, please accept this which I hold dear, as a token of my love and respect for you."*

I do not know the origins of this — it may be very old, or very modern — but the words are lovely anyway, and it was one of the first things I learned regarding ritual. It was the first time I had ever used someone else's words, but I have never forgotten them and have spoken them hundreds of time.

May they serve you well.

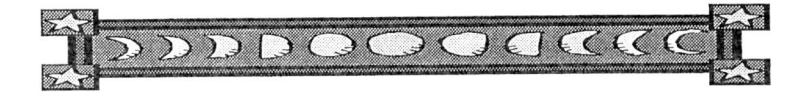

THE FIRE TIDE
May—The Hare Moon

The very name of this moon brings to mind thoughts of magic and sorcery, and is an ideal time of year for witches to begin weaving their charms and spells.

One old custom which is still practised today is that of making rowan crosses of protection. These consist of two small twigs of rowan, each with a little groove cut out so that they fit together. These are then bound in a criss-cross pattern with scarlet thread or wool; a loop is woven as the thread fills the cross so that the charm can be hung above a doorway.

In the past, farmers used to hang rowan crosses above barn and stable doors to prevent bewitchment of cattle and horses, but I believe the custom dates farther back than people think. To be afraid of bewitchment one would have to be christian, and one of the favourite accusations levelled at those suspected of witchcraft was when a horse was found to be lathered and weary in its stable. The unfortunate animal was said to have been 'hag-ridden'; that is to say that the owner suspected that it had been taken by witches and ridden furiously across the skies, no doubt accompanied by demons, if not the devil himself. On a more practical level, there is a strong possibility that some of these unfortunate animals were suffering from colic, which can induce profuse sweating and extreme discomfort in horses, leaving them looking raddled.

Although it is not beyond the realms of possibility that some animals may actually have been 'borrowed' for the night. Leaving out the more fanciful aspects, it is reasonable to consider that someone wanting to go about their business in the night, perhaps to some secret meeting several miles away, might easily have borrowed a neighbours horse to ease the journey. Horses are quite adept at picking their way in the dark, and for the sheer enjoyment of it, I have been known to disappear onto the moors at midnight; it is an exhilarating experience, I assure you. Wild animals do not bolt for cover as they do if a human is on foot, and I have spent many happy nights roaming about, safe in the knowledge that I could gallop away from anyone if the need had arisen. Perhaps some of those 'hag-ridden' horses had been borrowed by the local wise woman to tend the sick, or deliver a baby?

There is usually an element of truth behind old superstitions, and I see no reason why *some* of these animals could not have been genuinely 'hag-ridden. After all, if a witch urgently needed a herb which only grew ten miles away, how else could it be gathered under the full moon? Having said that, I suspect colic would have been the correct diagnosis in the majority of cases.

Hares and horses are often linked together in tales of shape-shifting, and the common denominator between both animals is that of speed. When watching hares in spring and autumn, racing and leaping, zig-zagging swiftly over the furrows and downs, we can only be impressed by their speed and agility. So it is with the horse, and especially horses and ponies running wild. There is no wonder that these animals have become so firmly woven into our folk-lore. For anyone wanting to travel swiftly over rough countryside, these two animals make fine choices if you are going to do it by shape-shifting.

Nowadays, a lot of people make the mistake of thinking that the art of shape-shifting is no more than a bit of play-acting: a sort of sacred dance which looks good but which doesn't really do anything magically. *POPPYCOCK!* When shape-shifting is done properly it involves us in the use of *extraordinary* magic.

The magic of this moon can be seen in two ways. There is the obvious fertility aspect regarding this moon (the hare is well known for it's fecundity), and another much deeper magical message. As we have already celebrated and done our bit as they say, regarding the fertility of spring and summer, we shall concentrate on the magic behind the Hare Moon, and the excitement of shape-shifting.

Here we combine the elemental tides of spring and summer. The earthy spring tide reflects the sensual, awaking 'serpent' energy with the impetus to send us flying in astral form, while the fire tide of summer represents sensuous heat and movement. Should anyone mistakenly believe earth tides to be being gentle, slow moving and still, should think about earth in another capacity. It can gush in torrents when introduced to water; it can erupt from the centre of the earth as molten larva. This is where the spirit of summer comes into its own, and this is how we see the rampant energy of the god, manifesting in the abundant growth of all things natural.

Another wonderful way of seeing two elements working together is to watch a farrier shoeing a horse, for when the blazing hot shoe is plunged into the bucket, the cold water almost explodes with energy. It boils furiously, and the resulting liquid is then aptly called 'thunder water'. This is a prized ingredient to a witch and I would advise anyone to make an effort to procure some.

My local blacksmith is quite used to me asking him for this, and as a great deal of magic still surrounds this skill, most farriers will not turn a hair at your request. This same man has made magical tools for me in the past and, without a lot being said, I think we understand each other pretty well.

The art of shape-shifting is one of the five old skills which marked a witch. The others being divining, summoning, hexing and healing (both sides of the same coin) and 'telling the maze'. It is because we are attempting to understand the Hare Moon, that we are going to look into shape-shifting.

One of the most difficult parts about writing about this, is the fact that it is very difficult to put into words the actual *essence* of magic. This is as it should be, because after all magic is elusive and not of this world, so perhaps that is part of the reason why true magical traditions do not work with the written word so much as by example.

You can only *fully* understand something magical when you have experienced it for yourself. This is why I have tried to suggest ways in which you can experience these things, as opposed to merely reading about them. For those among you who will only read this book for curiosity's sake, there may not be much to gain. For others, I hope it will have become clear that the moons need to be really *worked* through, in order to get the full understanding of what they impart.

The main difference between reading this, or any magical book, and actually working with it, is a matter of faith — a faith in your *own* abilities, not mine. Absolute faith is essential and for anyone genuinely drawn to the mysteries of the old path, these abilities can be startling. You are only limited by your *own* self-doubt, and these are things which should have been left well behind during the work of the Storm Moon.

The art of shape-shifting depends almost entirely on the level of affinity one develops with the animal world. It is popularly believed that this affinity should be linked to one particular animal or creature, which is now commonly referred to in shamanic terms as your 'totem' animal. In actual fact there are some very salient points about totem animals which seem to be overlooked these days.

It is not always a good idea to think that we choose our totem animals. It would be far more honest to say that they choose *us*. What this animal will be can only be discovered by a lot of careful thought and exploration. We should first consider which creature seems to have played a major and on-going part in our lives. Just because you have a pet cat does not necessarily mean that the cat is your totem.

Think about any life changing events which may have occurred to you and try to remember whether there was any particular animal involved. This may not necessarily be in its physical form, it could be more a case of what the creature symbolically represents. Many of the magical insights we receive are sent in symbolic form and it is essential to develop a sensitivity to this as magic is rarely cut and dried.

The determining of your particular animal or creature is something which everyone must find for themselves and is not something which can be directed by anyone else. It would be a good idea to refresh your memory about the magic of the earlier moons by devising a short ritual to assist you in finding the animal helper who is akin to you.

At an appropriate time, take your charm of protection to a place which is special to you and where you won't be disturbed. Cast the circle and then focus your concentration inwards by chanting some words of power to yourself. These words of power are best spoken from the heart but I will offer an example of the sort of thing to be aiming for:

*By the powers that be, let me see,
my animal friend, who stands by me.*

Now picture yourself walking alone through the woods and fields. Try to recreate a favourite walk but see this happening in the early morning when you will not encounter anyone else. As you walk farther away into the distance, keep listening and watching for something to show itself. There is no need to be nervous, if you hear noises just keep walking calmly, your animal friend will reveal itself sooner or later. Even if you would normally be afraid to encounter this particular creature in its physical form (i.e. a snake, hawk or bat) you must keep remembering that in its magical form this is your true ally and *will not* harm you.

In all truthfulness, very often it takes a bit of a fright to kick the magic into gear, so if you do meet something which scares you, stand still but do not lose your concentration. Hold tight to your charm of protection and wait. If you are in any danger, your animal protector will certainly come to your aid and, with an experience like this, you will be left in no doubt about what it is that walks with you as your friend.

As I have said before, real witchcraft is not all sweetness and light, and it is often when we are feeling at our most vulnerable and frightened that our true guardians appear. Do not forget that all creatures are under the protection and law of our gods, and in some ways they are a representation of them. The Ol' Lad has a wicked sense of humour and he will no doubt have a bit of sport with you before the day is out. In some ways these experiences are ways of testing us. A milksop witch cannot serve the gods of nature, because we all know what happens to the weak. They become a tasty morsel to the strong.

Once an animal friend, or familiar, has shown itself to you on the other planes, you can then make an effort to get to know all that you can about its habits on the physical level. Not only will this understanding strengthen the bond between you, but it is vital if you want to shape-shift into this particular type of animal. For instance, it will be no good trying to run like the wind as a rabbit, if you have no idea how rabbits run at full tilt. You must study the movements and habits, down to the finest detail. Take note of any seasonal changes in the creature's coat or plumage, and note whether its habitat changes. Try to learn all you can, right down to how the creature smells.

No tiny detail should be overlooked as being insignificant, however mundane it seems to be. This is why it is impractical for *you* not to decide that you want a more exotic creature as your totem if you will not encounter it *naturally*, albeit in symbolic form during your daily life. To follow the path of the natural witch, it is necessary to interact with creatures that are native to your landscape.

Having established a strong bond with your familiar (for this is what it truly is), you can begin to experiment with *becoming it*. Return to your magical circle and put out your call. After a few minutes your familiar will come. Gaze into its eyes and gently begin to exchange minds.

It is important to remember that this exchange is every bit as risky for your familiar as it is for you. After all, you are leaving your body for a temporary dwelling place in his/hers, and it is important that you place yourself in a sacred and protected area first. This is why there have been accounts of some witch being hounded and persecuted over hills and dales, yet when the hunters have shot or trapped the victim, they have only been able to find an injured or dead animal where the body should have been.

Perhaps this explains why such a thorough knowledge of your surroundings and the creatures in it is so important. You should check out the possibility of traps and snares in the area, not to mention poachers and gamekeepers. It stands to reason that when we shape-shift, we do not lose our physical body entirely and, as a result, there is a slight risk of injury which will obviously leave its mark on our body - which will become apparent when you return to it. These things may sound like fanciful imaginings, but I *know* from experience that it is so.

Having a natural bond with animals and especially those of my own with whom I spend all day, I have always been blessed with a natural inclination towards shape-shifting — and there is at least one occasion when I believe it has saved me from danger. One autumn evening I was making my way back from my horses and, as it was getting late and bordering on being dark, I decided to cut through a small spinney at the edge of the fields rather than follow the footpath by the road. The spinney itself was welcoming enough but I had not banked on encountering another human being there.

I had been spending about twenty-two hours a day with a mare who had been having problems. I had bought her as a bargain at auction and, lovely though she was and physically in good shape, she had been frightened so badly that she was extremely nervous of people. Day and night I'd persevered gently, even confining her to a stable where I had slept in the straw with her. At last I was being rewarded by her trust and a bond had developed between us. In fact, this particular mare and I eventually became so close that we often used to sneak up onto the moors together. With no bridle or saddle, I would hop on her back and gallop with complete confidence. We communicated telepathically and even though she was always a nervous animal, she never once put either of us in any danger.

This particular evening I was in a happy and relaxed state of mind, thrilled with the progress my mare was making. She had been watered, fed and in a secure paddock with her companions; I was looking forward to getting home to a hot bath and a good meal. As I hurried through the darkening evening I suddenly picked up a noise with my inner sense and peering towards it, could just make out the shape of a man semi-hidden in a disused gateway. He was staring intently at me and not moving at all: the message was one of grave danger.

Without a split second's thought I leaped out towards the field, my feet floating almost as if I were galloping away. My breath came easily and without even thinking about it, I headed for the thick hawthorn hedge which bordered the field. Gauging my take-off perfectly I stood back and leaped clean over the hedge and away down the next field. I will never forget the exhilaration of sailing easily over the five foot barrier as though it was nothing. I carried on over the next field before I began to tire yet when I did pull up, I was barely out of breath. This feeling of exhilaration stayed with me all evening, after I realised what I'd done.

This was a fine example of spontaneous shape-shifting, which had no doubt been activated by sheer fear. My nervous reaction to the man must have been exactly the same as that in my mare, and our closeness had consequently made the shift occur naturally.

It did occur to me to wonder just what the man must have thought, because one minute there was a girl walking alone through a wood and the next second she'd taken off at an amazing speed, jumping a hedge which no human being in their right mind would have tackled. Not only jumped it, but cleared it with inches to spare as well. This is just one simple example of how shape-shifting can be a powerful protection to a witch.

Not everyone, of course, has a natural talent for this type of magic but it is something that should be attempted by anyone seriously hoping to work the old arts. The ability to leave our bodies and assume other shapes is a liberating experience; it can open up so many possibilities and lead to so many adventures that it is well worth some concentrated time and effort. Patience is a virtue, but do not be surprised if your first success happens by accident. It is often the case with magic, we may need a bit of a jolt to take us out of everyday mode, but if our protection and faith is strong we survive.

Do not forget to leave a thank you to the wild creatures for this type of gift, even a tin of dog or cat food tipped out on the grass in the fields will be appreciated. Whether you run with the hare or the horse, or any other creature, always show respect and appreciation for these are our friends, and I believe that this is something of the magic of the Hare Moon.

Because I have referred to your animal friend as being a 'familiar', perhaps I had better explain a little about them. If you want to be technical, an animal helper (nowadays called a totem) is not always the same as a familiar, but a witch who is a proper working witch will usually simply have a familiar who accompanies him or her in magical workings. This familiar is whatever you want it to be, though they do very often appear in animal forms.

Occasionally, they may dwell in a special pet who may have a somewhat eccentric personality, but often they remain in elemental form. They need a home or base in which they are 'housed' and this can be a living animal, or it can be a small box, a stone, a piece of jewellery or an ornament. This may be something which would normally be on your altar if you have one, or it could be kept in a quiet place in the house.

It is usual to expect your familiar to do some specific job at which it can excel, like guarding the home, or yourself, but if you need different tasks doing, it is probably easier to have several. One word of caution, like pets and children, they need looking after, so do not saddle yourself with too many to care for at once.

There is a recognised method of enlivening a familiar and this was passed on to me many years ago. Therefore I can offer it here with the utmost confidence that it works and that it's genuine. An inner disquiet prevents me from offering the rite word for word, but I will give the method and hope that your instincts will guide you to knowing what to say.

Sit quietly within your sacred circle, your familiar (or a representation of it) in there with you. Before you there should be a flame, some water, some incense and a bowl of earth to represent the four elements. Build the power up within yourself until you can see a steady stream running from your hands. Taking your familiar in your hands, pass it through the incense smoke, saying a charm to bring to it the power of intellect, in other words, you are giving it the power to think for itself and understand your words. Next, you pass it across the flame, again doing the same with a charm, but this time you are giving it 'will', which will give it incentive and drive.

Next, work through the water element, and finally touch it to the earth to ground all these qualities into its body. Finally, you should give it one big blast of your witch-power and this, in effect, brings him/her to life, complete with all the elemental qualities. Now devise a command to awaken him/her, and a command to close down to sleep. In this way you retain control over him/her (as long as you're sensible) because an out of control familiar can become dangerous, not only to you but to itself. Naturally this is only done with a representation—a family pet would certainly not appreciate your efforts!

Now that you have a living, working familiar before you, for which you have a responsibility; it must be fed, and be given a life span. This latter is a vital requirement, because if anything should happen to you suddenly, you do not want a lost and 'motherless' familiar running around distractedly. There is a recipe for spirit food which is common sense, but if you like you can programme your familiar to simply take what he needs (within reason!) from your aura. Do be wary with this method, because although it saves you the trouble, it does smack of laziness.

A lazy witch needs eyes in the back of her head, as any familiar with some 'nous' as they say, will quickly take advantage. Spirit food usually consists of milk, bread and honey, and sometimes a *drop* of brandy when a familiar has done an especially good job. Do be careful with the alcohol, as I once went a bit overboard with the port and ended up with a non-functioning familiar.

Familiars certainly develop very definite characters of their own, and there may even come a time when they will play you up. If this starts to be a real problem you should close him down awhile and stop all food. However, much the same as we let our children have a certain amount of free rein, you should not turn into a tyrant. Common sense in all things, even magical things. Try to be a good 'guardian' and you should be amply rewarded.

May you travel together safely.

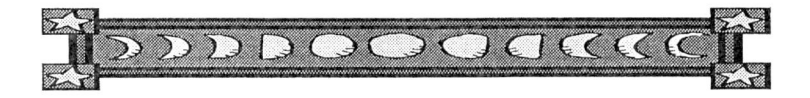

THE FIRE TIDE
June—The Honey Moon

This is one of the few old moon names which has survived in our everyday speech. As the name implies, this time has to do with marriages, unions and the recognition that as a result of the perfect union, the survival of life is ensured. At the summer solstice we see a perfect union in the day and the night; a perfect balance in time and, as witches, we feel and honour it. In our simple celebrations we are offering our blessings on this union. That it may remain harmonious throughout the natural world, not only on our earthly level, but on a cosmic level too.

Honey Moon also makes us think of bees and at this time of the year they are very busy. Our ancestors would have gone out into the woods and risked considerable discomfort to raid the honey from the bees. And it was probably with the eye of a hunter that they first noticed the intricate social system of bees — which is not unlike that of a coven of witches.

Bees have long been sacred to us, so it is worth trying to understand a little about their ways. They are wonderful little creatures, who respond well to kindness and a calm approach. I am fortunate to have a colony of wild bees living in an old wall in a part of the garden we cultivate as little as possible. Bees get along fine with humans, as long as we let them alone to live a quiet life.

Instinctively 'my' bees, sense that I respect them. Many a time I've picked up a tired bee and taken it indoors to revive. Placed in a matchbox on a leaf, with a tiny drop of honey to sustain them, I eventually have the pleasure of seeing most of them perk up enough to fly home.

Even though I have a severe allergy to stings and bites, 'my' bees seem to return my offer of friendship and protection. On more than one occasion when I've been sitting quietly under the trees reading a book, a bee has landed on my bare arm and had a good wash and brush up. Some of them have even crawled into the crook of my arm to curl up to sleep. This means I'm forced to sit quite still for as long as it takes a bee to have forty winks but then that's not such a difficult thing to do on a warm summer's day, is it?

The natural laws of the bee's life cycle are similar to that of a working coven to such an extent that I am inclined to believe that witches of old must have studied this intently. Even the sacrificial male, having mated with the Queen, is part of the bee's social structure - and the comparisons continue in lots of other ways. There are three classes of bee in a hive: the Queen, the drones and the workers. The Druid system has the Druids, the Ovates and the Bards, while within the modern coven system many groups follow a system based on achieving three levels or degrees.

Bee keeping is one of our oldest rural traditions simply because for thousands of years mankind has recognised the wonderful healing properties of honey. Not to mention the magic of propolis, which is another creation by the bees. Both honey and propolis should be 'standard issue' in any witch's kitchen and is available from any good herbalist.

On a practical note, it is a good idea to begin saving any empty jars and containers that can be used to store dried herbs, resins, and anything to contain ointments, liniments, salves etc. I am afraid my home is bursting at the seems with jars, bottles and pots, in every shape colour and size. Some of these are very old, while others are modern, but each one has been kept with a purpose in mind. Some are kept for the colour alone, others because they are decorative or intriguing. If I can fit a shelf in a space, I will fill it with bottles!

Some are already filled with magical potions, some are there 'just in case'. A working witch is always well prepared, and even if we haven't any specific purpose in mind, a goodly assortment of odd jars and bottles helps to bring a bit of quaintness into our homes. Quite simply, they remind us of magic; they help us to *feel* like witches, when all around us the modern world runs around chasing its own tail and getting nowhere.

Once you start herb gathering, you will be amazed at just how much stuff you can land up collecting. Be prepared to put those new shelves up! You have only to read a good herbal to see the vast array of herbs and plants we can utilise; not forgetting that from any one plant, we may be able to call upon four or five different uses.

Let's take the elder as a prime example. This wonderful tree isn't called the 'poor man's medicine chest' for nothing. From this one tree alone we can gather flowers, berries, leaves, bark *and* the particular fungus which grows on the trunk. There is certainly nothing wasted from the elder tree because added to this are the *magical* properties, which could inspire you to create magical potions of your own.

I always gather as much from the elder as possible, much of it from my own garden. In winter, when coughs and sniffles are common, there is no finer cure-all than a hot toddy made from elder flowers and sweetened with pure honey. Even though the blossoms have a distinctive smell not unlike a visiting tomcat while they are drying, they make a surprisingly pleasant tea when infused in hot water.

Nowadays it is possible to purchase elderflower cordial from most big supermarkets if you cannot harvest your own herb. Drunk cold, with a slice of lemon, it makes a delicious and refreshing change from orange squash. Mixed with piping hot water in winter, it will drive out a cold in next to no time.

The loose dried flowers can also be tied up in a muslin bag and hung on the hot tap of the bath. At the first sign of a cold, run a hot bath with elderflower and take a hot drink of the same into the bath with you. After a good, hot soak, climb into a nice warm bed and enjoy a deep refreshing sleep. During the night you will sweat the cold away and, nine times of out ten, all symptoms will have disappeared by the morning.

Without detracting from all the wonderful qualities of the elder, a proportion of the remedy's effectiveness can be put down to the use of honey used as the sweetener. Honey is a complete food in itself, and it is also very easily digested and assimilated. It consists mostly of glucose and levulose — and glucose is the source of energy that our bodies prefer. In times of illness, when we are under considerable strain, honey can be absorbed into our system more easily than other forms of sugar, because it does not need to be broken down by our digestive tracts. This gives an ailing body less work to do so that it can benefit from the action of the honey so much more quickly.

Surprisingly honey contains much more than most of us give it credit for, including enzymes and minerals, including calcium, phosphorous, sulphur, sodium, potassium, magnesium, iron, chlorine and iodine salts. In certain types of honey there can also be manganese, silicon, aluminium, chromium, boron, copper, lithium, nickel, zinc and osmium, all of which are important in maintaining a healthy bloodstream.

Honey is an alkaline substance which can help to balance our normally acidic systems, yet conversely it contains many organic acids which help increase the activity in our bodies, thus assisting us to heal. As if this list wasn't impressive enough, honey also contains the vitamins B2 B6 H K and C, with the darker coloured honeys being the richest in mineral content. Nowadays with pollution affecting such a large portion of the world it is worth investing in the best honey that you can.

A lot of the honey sold in supermarkets has been heat treated to keep it fluid during transit, but unfortunately this effectively strips it of most of its nutrients, therefore cheap honey is basically useless except as a flavouring agent. A good honey should still contain strong antibacterial properties, and all honey is a powerful natural disinfectant, which makes it wonderful for healing wounds as well as being the perfect partner to herbal preparations aimed at curing many types of illness.

It is this natural partnership which Nature demonstrates so perfectly during this moon. Here are the bees, working in a perfect harmony with the plants, in order to produce honey, which in turn draws from those plants certain healing agents we can use to restore health. It is a simple and natural example of the god and goddess energies in perfect balance, at a time when the tides of moon and sun are also in perfect harmony.

This partnership between honey and our healing herbs is not merely a fanciful and romantic description, it is truly a magical marriage. The action of honey, when combined with herbs, is one of harmonising and balancing, thus creating a brew which will react in perfect harmony with the body's requirements, to bring about a swift and balanced recovery.

Many modern treatments have all manner of side effects, and while they might tackle the obvious cause of the problem, the body is put under yet more pressure as it tries to counterbalance them. The action of herbs and honey on an illness or wound, is one which acts in sympathy with the body, thus treating it gently and with encouragement. We can effect a marvellous cure, yet without putting our bodies under any more strain.

When it comes to choosing the perfect honey, I recommend a product called Manuka honey which comes from New Zealand. It is a little bit more expensive than other types but the cost is amply justified by its amazing power. This is an opaque honey with a rich flavour, and a soft toffee-like texture, and I can personally vouch for its wonderful effectiveness. It is a prime example of that old saying "you get what you pay for" and this is an investment which every witch should try to add to the herb cupboard.

Coincidentally, as I was writing this chapter, I got into conversation with a retired gentleman who was telling me about Greek honey. After a triple heart by-pass operation, he was advised to take Greek honey every day, on the assurance that it would clear any fluid from his chest. Suffice to say that he took the advice, and is so impressed with the results, that he has just booked a holiday to Greece, with the intention of bringing lots of honey back with him. He looks and feels great, and the proof of the pudding is in the eating as they say.

So perhaps we should all consider having some Greek honey on the shelf as well, and by now you will be appreciating what I meant when I said that we witches end up with lots of bottles and shelves!

Nowadays, much of what passes as witchcraft is nothing more than a form of nature-based christianity, in that its members simply turn up for a gathering, worship a deity, then have a social supper before going home again. *This is not witchcraft,* and it quite makes my blood boil, that people without any of the old skills, pass themselves off as authorities on Craft working.

To truly be a witch of *any* calibre you should not only master the magical old arts of shapeshifting, divination and casting spells, but also the *practical* arts of 'wort law' and birthing, not to mention a rudimentary knowledge of laying out the dead. These things are what *life is all about.* It is not enough merely to stand under the moon making pretty speeches about revering life. We must *know* how to nurture life in the practical sense otherwise our devotions are absolutely meaningless — not only to us, but to the gods themselves. This is why herbal knowledge is so important,; for herbs are the natural medicines which the gods themselves have given us, in order that we can remain fit and healthy.

What a slap in the face it must be to them, when people claim to love them, yet reject their gifts to mankind in favour of artificially created tablets which can do more harm than good. What good is it expecting the old gods to take care of us, if we won't even learn from them how to take care of ourselves?

The month of the Honey Moon is an ideal time to strike a balance against all the inner temple work which has been the basis of the first three moons.

Now is the time for some *practical* stuff and, with the re-emergence of the bees and the plants, it is a good time to start perfecting your 'wort cunning'. Begin by investing in a pair of rubber or cotton gardening gloves, because one of the first plants to look for is the common or garden, stinging nettle.

This is not because it is any more magical than any other herb or plant, but just simply because absolutely everyone can find and recognise one. (Even if this *is* done the hard way) Treat yourself to a thoroughly good herbal with clear illustrations, and have a look locally to see what you are certain of recognising. You may be surprised how many different things you will find as you go out and about your everyday life. While many herbs and plants will be available to you on the road side, these are not suitable for picking. They will be saturated by pollution, and possibly quite toxic. Head for the quiet places, the farther away the better from roads and traffic. Even those growing on cultivated farmland could have been sprayed with invisible chemicals, so it really *is* worth making the effort to gather things from remoter regions whenever possible.

The nettle is a good one to start with because apart from being unmistakeable, it is so prevalent that everyone should be able to find a patch. Added to this, nettles need to be picked when they are young, pale green and tender, which means that they can be chosen very early in the season, unlike many plants which need to be harvested later in the year. There is also a good reason for nettles being gathered when young, and this is because this is the time when they are most beneficial to us.

Come high summer, towards the end of June, beginning of July, the makeup of the nettle changes due to alterations in the soil, making them not only tough, but very laxative and, in fact, quite toxic. So although they begin life as being beneficial, they go on to make a subtle shift, which actually makes them baneful. This is just another little tide of life to note, and effectively displays the constant shifting and flowing throughout nature with which the natural witch is attuned.

From the humble nettle you can make up a tonic, rich in iron, a tasty soup, a dainty vegetable, a wonderful beer, a powder to sprinkle across your doorstep to stop unwanted visitors, a powder to summon lightening; from the roots you could twist a cord to use as a binding, and from the older, darker leaves you could make a pretty green dye.

These are just *some* of the ways in which the nettles can come to your aid. So always harvest them with respect, for these common plants found rambling over our fields and waysides, often have a lot more strings to their imaginary bows than many people believe. Think about that.

There have been all manner of complicated rituals and rigmaroles attached to the act of gathering herbs, and in a way I can see how the need has arisen for them. Nowadays many people cannot equate behaving with reverence towards something, unless they have words and actions that somehow differ from the norm. But reverence comes from the heart, and an understanding of the herbs and plants you are taking can be the first act of reverence.

'Wort cunning' is a vast area, requiring some serious study and effort, which may mean giving up something you normally do to relax, in order to concentrate on acquiring this knowledge. This type of effort and dedication, done in the spirit of truly desiring to learn in order to serve is the *true sacrifice*. It is not enough to glance through 'Culpeper' now and again and learn a few correspondences by rote, you must work with the plants until you can *feel* what they are suited to. Who knows? Perhaps you may come up with different correspondences to the revered Nicholas - and who is to say that yours are not every bit as valid?

Another aspect to consider when working with plants and herbs, is the effect of the sun and the moon on them. While the sun provides the fuel to make them grow, it is actually the pull of the moon's power which draws them up from the earth. This again is not mere fancy; those who really understand the ways of nature, plant seeds under a waxing moon.

Looking deeper into this, we can see that this is another way of nature showing us clearly that the path to the Goddess *is* through the Horned God. For through the actions of the sun, which provides the strength for the plant to grow; it is the lunar power which actually draws them out to where we can harvest them. Clearly, without the gifts of the god, there would be nothing tangible for us to receive from the Goddess. And so our actions on this physical plane, reflect our progress in the spiritual one.

This is what I mean when I say that it is not enough to simply worship the Goddess, and it is certainly *not enough* to make pretty speeches under the moon. There must be a balance in everything we do, on all levels, and there is no more appropriate time to consider these things, than at the time of the Honey Moon.

Unless you are a rapid learner, however, do not attempt to

gather everything and anything that takes your fancy just for the sake of it. You will probably end up with a pile of withered leaves, which you can't identify. Instead, harvest two or three types which you *are* certain of, and then proceed to learn as much as you possibly can about them. These will become imprinted on your mind, and the following year you can do the same again, until you have a sound understanding of a sensible range. You will not need to scrabble for any books in order to make up a potion to cure the sick — and you will be well on the way to being *a proper* witch in the old tradition.

Another of the commonest and most useful things to gather is that good old enemy of the gardener: chickweed. When it is rich, green and lush in summer, I always gather a huge supply which I hang up in small bunches above the fire to dry. Rich in Vitamin C which makes it an excellent addition to any cold remedy, and the young tender fresh leaves can be added to summer salads. Not only is it a tasty change, but it also helps ward off those infuriating summer colds to which we sometimes fall prey.

As well as a cold cure, it also makes an excellent salve for chapped hands, and with a drop of lavender oil, it has been known to clear stubborn eczema in a matter of days. For all skin complaints it is a safe and gentle, yet effective remedy, and a few pots of salve are always part of my apothecary. I always think that the tiny white flowers with which it is clothed, are a certain sign that the Lady smiles on this herb, and it is definitely one of my favourites. Common 'weeds' such as chickweed should not fool you with their humble abundance, it is no chance that the most common ones are often the most useful. Why else would Mother Nature ensure that we have a plentiful supply.

In the majority of cases, we will not need vast collections of exotic and exciting sounding ingredients in order to build up an effective apothecary, because many herbs and plants have very similar properties and actions. From a collection of a dozen or so well preserved healthy herbs, we can actually tackle most everyday ailments. Perhaps nature offers us such a wide diversity so that anyone living in any region, can have access to plants which do similar jobs. Again, the tides of life come into play because this wide diversity also takes into account the changing seasons. In other words, just because we are in the depths of winter, it doesn't mean that we cannot find a bark or root which can do the very same job as a tender spring leaf.

In honouring these tides, however, it is as well to consider the Earth Mother herself. It is wise to gather and utilise as much as we can while her bounty is being freely given, for just as giving birth to a baby is hard work, the effort of birthing all the abundance of summer is hard work, and our 'mother' needs her rest through the winter months. Try to work in harmony with her, and honour her resting period without impatience, safe in the knowledge that she will provide again when she is refreshed.

This is why our ancestors saw the summer tide as belonging to the Goddess, and the winter tide belonging to the God. We need to work differently in winter, and just like any responsible parents, the gods each have their roles to play in nurturing us, their children — and just like children we, too, have an awful lot to learn.

BASIC SALVE METHOD

The simplest method of making up a salve is to use a big pot of petroleum jelly as your base. I have heard other people criticise this ingredient, but it is easy to work with, and the end result can be more or less guaranteed to be right. Some old recipes call for the use of lard as a base, which is fine if you do not need the salve to have a very long shelf life.

Another drawback with lard, is the fact that if it is applied regularly it has a tendency to cause hair growth. This is all well and good if you want to rub it on your head, but for other bits of our bodies it is usually an unwanted side effect.

Simmer the herbs you need in a pan (not aluminium) until they have absorbed most of the water. Just enough to cover them to start with will be plenty. When they are beginning to go crisp, remove from the fire (or heat) and pour the remaining concentrated liquid through a fine sieve into a container. Gently melt the petroleum jelly until it's all runny, then gradually mix in the herb extract. If you think this is going to be too runny, you can add a little beeswax to it all. Personally, I like the addition of wax, as it incorporates the magic of the bees into the salve.

Whip this all together until it's smooth, then pour into clean, dry, sterilized pots. Leave to cool before securing a lid. Label and date, then store in a cool place, out of direct sunlight.

This is only a very basic method, and with a bit of research you will find all manner of different methods and ingredients, with which you can experiment. The humble chickweed is a prince among weeds, so this is as good a place as any to start your magical collection.

"Beloved Pan, and all ye other Gods who haunt this place, give me beauty in the inward soul; and may the outward and inward man be as one."

Phaedrus, Plato

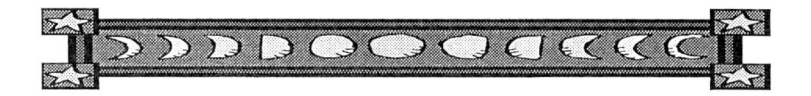

THE FIRE TIDE
July—The Mead Moon

This is one of my favourite names among the moons, and what better name could our forebears have thought of to describe the full blooded and joyous celebration of summer. The trees that burst into leaf during the Earth Tide are laden and the grass is lush, the flowers are beautiful, and the bees are busy from dawn till dusk, gathering their precious cargo, ready to produce their wonderful honey ... as the Fire Tide flows into the Air Tide, mead is seen as being representative of *all four* tides.

Which makes it the perfect time to have a go at brewing the wonderful old recipe for mead. Though this may not at first appear to be in keeping with the Water Tide, it certainly is appropriate because one vital ingredient of any home brew, is nice, clear water heated over Fire. We may take it for granted that the water we have supplied via the mains, is clear and fit to drink, but this hasn't always been the case. Although springs and streams were probably far cleaner than they are today, the wells were sometimes contaminated by vermin. A lot of the summer ailments like dysentery and typhoid used to be caused by unfit water supplies.

Water has always been recognised as being essential to life, and as soon as mankind discovered the art of brewing, these supplies of mead and wine would have been a very important aspect of the summer. What was made in the summer, had to be carefully stored to supply the needs of the village for an entire winter (Water Tide).

The combination of pure water and pure honey together (plus one or two other ingredients) makes a drink which is not only beautiful but beneficial as well. I have a suspicion that mead may have begun as a cure or preventative for the summer sicknesses which always ran rampant and, because it was also pleasurable to drink, it was perhaps made in increased quantities to sustain people over the winter too. Whoever said that medicine had to taste nasty for it to do any good, had obviously never tasted a good mead. Mind you, I have been guilty of saying the same, especially when trying to persuade my family to drink some of my herbal cures!

Not all our cures and potions taste bad , but occasionally there will be cause to include a certain herb which, although doing an excellent job, happens to taste rather revolting. One such herb that immediately springs to mind is horehound, and the minute I hear that word I have to smile because it brings to mind a picture of an acquaintance of mine, who had me laughing heartily over her horehound tea diet.

It was after the birth of her son that she decided that those few extra pounds which we all gain, were just not going as fast as she'd hoped. Her husband remembered that horehound tea is reputed to assist weight loss, and without further ado began 'helping' by making her horehound tea morning, noon and night. One day she telephoned me to say that if she ever saw any more horehound tea she would leave the country. She complained bitterly about the flavour, and the fact that it left a ghastly after-taste which lasted ages. No doubt to put her right off what she was eating hence the link to weight loss. "So you must have lost lots then?" I asked. There was a hesitant "Erm, no." I finally winkled it out of her (when her husband was out of earshot) that the horehound tea was so horrible that the only way to get rid of the taste was to swiftly eat several chocolate biscuits! Needless to say, the tea-diet wasn't a roaring success.

At the end of the chapter I offer a recipe for mead, which in fact it comes from this very same person and, she assures me that it doesn't contain the slightest hint of horehound. It is always very satisfying to brew our own recipes and to use them in our celebrations, because they evoke memories of summer and of the magic we were feeling as we made them.

On a magical note, the Fire Tide is the perfect time to explore the magic of the sacred flame. The beach makes a wonderful setting for this very special bonfire, because the driftwood we need to collect for it has been soaked in brine. As a result, it produces fascinating flames in hues of blues and greens, purples and even sometimes, reds. This makes it perfect for divinatory work of a rather special nature. The beach is the point where land and sea unite, and this in itself creates a magic all its own. With the stars overhead, and the voices of the sea surrounding us, we have a ready-made setting for magic.

Damp sand is perfect for drawing a circle upon, and some incense sprinkled on the sacred fire makes a beautiful offering to the night sky. There is a very special feel to magic like this, because it is so illusive. It is as though we are welcomed temporarily into the magical realms of the sea and her magic — only to watch as all of our traces are washed away and all evidence of our being here removed.

At times like this, it is as though the goddess allows us to step into her world, knowing that the visit will only be a fleeting glimpse. When the tide turns and the sea covers the beach again, our magical energies will be re-absorbed back into the great womb, taking all traces of our circle back to its source. This gives us a poignant reminder that our magic is only ever borrowed, and that we must always be willing to let it return to the realms of nature.

During the day, try to locate a suitable spot to which you can return easily at night, but do *check the times of the tides diligently.* To be on the safe side, allow yourself an extra half and hour to be clear of the beach before the tide turns. That way you are not likely to get cut off by any unexpectedly swift-rising water. Take a good look at the beach and be certain that you can leave without having to cross any narrow channels. Safety is paramount, and talking to a local resident will probably help you decide on a suitable place. Spring tides rise higher than summer, but still make sure that you have taken all things in to consideration before venturing down there in the darkness.

It is also a good idea to scour the area during the day for driftwood; if you pile it up among the rocks, no one is likely to disturb it. Build your fire (remembering to take something to start it with), then draw your circle around the fire, leaving enough space for you to walk around and sit comfortably. Depending on how adventurous you are feeling, this rite is especially potent when undertaken at the dark of the moon. This is the traditional time for magic related to the realms of mystery: the time to dip a magical toe into sorcery and ancient secrets.

Many well-known authors have stated that the dark of the moon is a time to be avoided magically. I (and many like me) find these claims disappointing to say the least. The dark of the moon is the time for working real old witchcraft, as the opportunity is there for making those Otherworld connections. If the idea of meeting old witches in the underworld frightens people, then they have no right to call themselves a witch in the first place! Summer Solstice is the time for this, as William Shakespeare well knew when he wrote *A Midsummer Night's Dream*.

To accompany a rite such as this, it is appropriate to take a special drink (called a philtre). As your home made mead will not be ready to drink, you may have to rely on buying a bottle. Before setting off, make up an infusion of vervain (5g in 100mls water). Let this cool before transferring into a flask, and pack this together with the mead and something suitable to eat. You might also like to take your notebook and a pen, to make notes of what you see in the flames. Before you commence, bathe your hands and face in this infusion, keeping a little back to add to the mead.

When the fire is blazing and the circle cast, sit comfortably and gaze into the fire as you sip your potion. The vervain will help to open your mind to magical energies—and who knows what wonderful things may be revealed in this perfect setting. When it is time to leave, throw the last remaining drops of liquor into the dying fire, and leave some food on dry land. This way you are honouring both the land and the sea. We do not close down a circle like this in the physical form, instead just leave the fire and the circle as they are and let the sea take them back into herself.

This kind of magic has a strange drawing power, and you will need to be vigilant about watching the tide. Even though there may be an element of danger in this kind of practice, it is something I would recommend you to try if the opportunity presents itself and you truly want to experience old magic.

One way of holding on to some of the night's magic is to take a clean container to the beach. As you come away from this sacred space, keep your eyes open for a rock pool. With a sense of reverence, fill your container with some of the water, so that you can use it in future rituals. Bathing your hands and face with a few drops each time will evoke the mysteries of the dark moon, and the sacred flame of the fire will burn again in your heart. Or you may use it as a scrying philtre in future magical operations.

There is no need to feel as though you shouldn't take it because it is virtually impossible to 'steal' water. One way or another it will find its way back to its source one day, so you are only borrowing it in a good cause. Do check though that there are no fish in it, as these will die if taken away from their natural habitat. Keep this sacred filter in a cool dark, secret place when you get home, and whenever you want to call up the power of water, you can pour some into a suitable vessel.

Because this water has such strong goddess associations, this might be a good time to keep an eye out for a pretty goblet, which can be your cup. This is also a powerful goddess symbol, and along with a sacred knife, is something which all witches will have and treasure. As with the knife, there is an unwritten rule about the way this should be obtained, and this, again, involves *never, ever haggling*.

When you do find the perfect items, that look and feel right, be prepared to 'pay' whatever it takes to get them. To do otherwise is a slight to the gods, and one over which they will take extreme offence. This same rule applies to any magical tools you purchase. The cup and the knife are symbols of the god and goddess, which is why we often dip the knife blade into the wine chalice in our rituals and ceremonies, as a symbol of the unity of the spirit. This is what the popular books refer to as the ceremony of 'the drawing down the moon'.

Your cup should be cleansed, consecrated and kept wrapped in a clean cloth so that it retains its special feel. Later in the year, when your mead is ready to drink, you will enjoy the magic of sharing your magical potion from your sacred chalice. When you pour your libation back into the earth, you will be sharing a deeply magical and private moment alone with the gods. Take your time and appreciate this, because it is a very beautiful magic.

On the subject of libations, it is always nice to make something special to have with the wine or mead, and here we can attune to the solar aspect of the duality. As the wine is to the Goddess, so the food is to the Horned God, and with this in mind I always try to bake something which is wholesome and natural. It does not need to be a wonderful culinary creation (which is a good thing in my case!) but a bit of thought on the matter should direct you towards making something suitable. If possible try to buy organic ingredients, and watch out for old recipes because many also contain honey.

The following are a few recipes from my own collection, most of which were my grandmother's (yes ... I know it's all been said before, but in this case it happens to be perfectly *true*). There's a vast difference between preserving family notes on old country herbals and recipes, and claiming that Granny was a witch. My Granny *was* a past master of country-lore but if you'd called her a witch, she'd have probably fetched you one with her stick!

All the measures are given just as they were written and if you want to convert them into metric, you must do this yourself. I am too old to bake in anything other than ounces and pounds!

OAT CRUNCHY
5oz. Butter
5oz. Sugar
6oz. Oats
A dessertspoon clear honey.
A good pinch of salt.

Melt the butter and sugar together in a large pan. When soft add all other dry ingredients and return to a low heat. Stir together and add the honey. When well combined, pour mixture into a shallow, greased oven-proof dish and bake in a slow oven till golden brown. When cool cut into squares and store in airtight tin.

ELDERFLOWER WINE

To every gallon of water put 2 lbs sugar. Boil for ½ hour and when lukewarm add ½ pint elder flowers, picked clean from the stalks. Add the juice and thinly pared rind of one lemon, 1 lb chopped raisins and 1 teaspoon yeast. Pour into a barrel, stirring often for 2 or 3 days. When it has 'done working', stop it up. After adding a small bottle of brandy it will be ready for bottling in one month.

    A little note at the bottom of this recipe says; "*Constance didn't put any brandy*". So I presume my Great Aunt Constance passed on the recipe ... and was a little less adventurous than Granny. It is up to you who you follow!

ELDERFLOWER CHAMPAGNE

To every gallon of flowers add one gallon of water. Boil for 10 minutes. To every gallon of syrup add 3½ lbs sugar, a little cinnamon and thick root ginger. Boil for 20 minutes. Drain, cool and ferment with yeast sprinkled on a slice of bread. In 7 days, strain and bottle. Keep eye on bottles, when working they may explode. You have been warned!

MEAD

4lbs honey
1 gallon spring water
1 each large orange and lemon
1 cup grape juice
A little yeast

Boil water and honey till dissolved. Cool, add lemon and orange juice with rinds finely grated. Add yeast and stir well. Pour into a barrel and stop up. Place in a dark cupboard somewhere warm. Let air out occasionally but leave three months to work. Take off clear liquid and bottle. Ready in one week, but better if left a year.

A RECIPE FOR MEAD
Rosehip Mead / Sweet Melomel

A melomel is a fruit flavoured mead. This recipe uses 4 lbs of rosehips, picked fresh (during the Water Tide) and boiled for five to ten minutes. To speed up softening time, you can drop them in a bag (an old pillowcase is ideal) and bash them on a hard surface with a wooden mallet. When cool, mash them by hand and strain through butter muslin. To this add 4 lbs honey, 15g citric acid (or lemon juice) and yeast nutrient, stir till honey is dissolved.

When lukewarm, add the yeast and ferment as usual. For best results use a sherry yeast, and ferment as for a sherry, i.e., after the first racking (not before) have your fermenting vessel only seven eights full (not topped up right to the neck) and use an empty air lock, the end of which should be plugged with cotton wool. This way a small amount of air can work the liquor, but vinegar flies cannot get in. This helps to develop the sherry flavour. From this stage treat as usual mead.

METHAGLIN
Otherwise known as rocket fuel!

To make methaglin use 4 lbs honey, 1oz hops and ½oz root ginger to every gallon. Another version uses the same amount of honey, 2 cloves and a ¼ oz cinnamon bark or one eight of an oz caraway seeds. Marjoram, balm, mace, lemon and orange peel, and cinnamon are all included in standard mead recipes, but don't overdo them; a little goes a long way. These offer room for experiment with flavour for personal taste. When a combination has been chosen, make up as for any standard mead, following same instructions for fermenting etc.

A well-made mead is so delicious that you will be tempted to drink lots — so look up a good hangover cure. Tomato juice with Lea & Perrins sauce and a raw egg stirred in works wonders.

Besides drinking the beverages of the Mead Moon, it is a good time to attempt to do some scrying. It is better not to try to combine the two activities, otherwise you will only become convinced that your totem animal is a pink elephant!

There are many methods to use when scrying with water. You can use the cup within a circle, or you can simply use a bowl kept specifically for the purpose. You can look directly into a pool or stream, or you can use water poured onto a silver tray. Use your imagination, and just go with what works the best for you.

There are no right or wrong ways, and there really is no need for complicated rituals or incantations. However, if you find that reciting a charm of your making helps, then this should not be seen as anything to be ashamed of. We all need our rituals to a certain degree, and if we are attempting an unfamiliar sort of magic, then it can help to get into the mood 'when we do a bit of ritual'.

Many people confuse the word ritual with long winded ceremonies involving pre-learned speeches and precise actions. This is not particularly accurate, because a ritual is simply something that you do regularly for a specific reason. Cleaning our teeth morning and night is a ritual; catching the bus to work is a ritual; touching a lucky charm before choosing our lottery numbers is a ritual. Going shopping at the farmer's market every Friday at the same time each week is a ritual.

Hopefully this will manage to convey that the word 'ritual' is nothing to be afraid of and, if you find that you can scry wonderfully as long as you turn round three times and sit facing South, then that's fine. This is *your ritual* and it works for you - that's all that counts at this level.

" ... so much more is there paradise in the scent of the green leaves at evening and in the appearance of the sea and in the redness of the sky; and there came to me a certain vision of a real world about us all the while, of a language that was only secret because we would not take the trouble to listen to it and discern it."

A Secret In A Secret Place
Arthur Machen

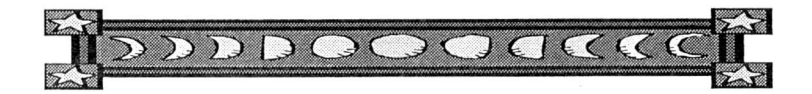

THE AIR TIDE
August——The Wort Moon

Summer is reaching her full power now, and nowhere is this more evident than in the abundance of fruit and crops in our hedgerows, fields and gardens. The tiny struggling shoots we smiled to see in spring, are now vigorous, rampant displays of the power of the Earth. Gifts from the gods are everywhere, from radiant flowers that move us with their beauty, to humble commonplace weeds. Although common, these should never be overlooked since many of these ordinary looking plants are the medicines we may need to fight winter ailments, and so should be considered with respect.

Take note too, of anything which suddenly grows in profusion close to where you live, for in the magical world nothing happens by sheer chance. The old gods took an opportunity to show me this truth very clearly some time ago.

My next door neighbour was an elderly chap, who liked nothing better than pottering about in his garden, either tending his carefully grown vegetables, or mowing his lawns. He had a lovely old fashioned garden, complete with two little green sheds in which he stored a myriad of implements and gadgets. His trees were pruned into tidy shapes, his tomatoes were a riot of reds and, with an old fashioned assortment of flowers crowding the beds, the garden had a magic all of its own. In fact, it was this old chap who, in those very sheds had a wonderful hand-worked machine on which he used to sharpen my magical knife. He always did this with the greatest respect and he is sadly missed.

There was an old essence about him and his garden, and I still have an old rose that he planted for his late wife, whom he loved dearly. Altogether I have very fond memories of them both and on his passing it was very sad to see the old garden being neglected.

Eventually, after a couple of summers with the cottage standing empty and in the throes of renovation, the garden became completely covered with feverfew. The family gave me free range to harvest as much as I liked and I wasted no time gathering great bunches and hanging them indoors to dry. I hadn't a clue what I was going to do with several pounds of dried feverfew, but I saw it as a gift and took it thankfully.

A year later we lost another elderly neighbour, and this time I inherited his dog. She is a dear little thing who settled in easily, but it soon became clear that she had a problem or two. In spite of having been very well cared for (in fact utterly spoiled would be more accurate), she had a nasty skin problem which, in spite of him spending hundreds of pounds at the vet's, just would not clear up. She was trimmed, bathed in expensive shampoo and kept on an anti-flea preparation but to no avail. She still tickled and scratched herself sore.

In desperation I gave up the concoction of tablets, and made her a hair tonic from feverfew. Several times a week I bathed her in feverfew and inside three weeks she was completely clear and happy again. Her coat is now rich and lustrous, and people stop me in the street to say how well she looks; even the vet is pleased for her.

I cannot put this all down to chance. It was a way of ensuring that I had the right herbs to hand to help this little dog. This was just one small example of how beautifully the Ol' Lad looks down on his creatures and tries to oversee their welfare.

Now that there is not such a pressing need for this herb, something else has taken over, and the feverfew is only growing in smaller clumps. The wind carried the seeds and it now grows in my garden. Just enough for my needs, and enough to confirm every year, that the Old Ones watch over us. It is the things like this which make me grateful that I am dedicated to them. It also serves to remind me of how little I know about 'life, the universe and everything' where the master plan is concerned and magic never ceases to amaze me.

And long may it be so.

The Wort Moon is sometimes called Lammas, or the Loaf Festival, because this is the time when the ripened corn is harvested. This precious cargo is transported to buildings, where it can be stored safely under cover, ready to supply the needs of the people throughout the long, cold winter. There are many folk traditions surrounding this time, the most famous being *John Barleycorn*. There *is* something particularly satisfying about making home made bread, and the aroma of it baking infuses the home with the spirit of the goddess of the hearth as nothing else can. While this corn/bread theme is an important part of our heritage, it is only one small part of the magic of this Moon and, as the name implies, we should also make an effort to gather and dry some of the wonderful medicines which are being offered to us now.

There are some quaint old associations regarding the gathering of herbs, and while a lot of them are wholly inappropriate in today's society, there are certain aspects which we can incorporate with a bit of imagination. For example: it would be fairly difficult for the majority of us to bath in a stream at dawn, before slipping into nothing but a white shift, and dancing barefoot round the herbs while chanting and waving a knife about. If I'd done that to gather my feverfew, I reckon that there could have been a few raised eyebrows and knowing looks, to say the least!

This doesn't mean that we cannot make our harvesting trips special. To make the above a bit more workable, I would content myself with having a normal bath or shower, dressing in a light summer outfit, and bathing my magical knife in my sacred scrying filter, or in some spring water sprinkled with salt. None of this is strictly vital but something along those lines does help to remind us that what we are doing is magical, and it is a mark of respect to the Old Ones, that we have made an effort to honour the occasion. The choice of herbs to collect depends entirely upon what you have growing to hand. In different parts of the country, certain things grow in profusion, while in others they may be scarce, or not grow there at all. One of the pleasure in knowing other witches from all over the country, is that you can always do a few swops.

Post each other a few seeds and we enhance our own herb bed.

I recommend that every would-be witch should invest in a good herbal, one with up-to-date descriptions and clear pictures. A copy of Nicholas Culpeper is lovely if you want a bit of guidance regarding planetary influences, but there are also a number of very easy-to-follow and reasonably priced books on making ointments, salves and perfumes currently in print.

Herb-lore is a vast and fascinating subject and if you gather a goodly selection of things this month, you'll have plenty to keep you supplied through winter. Try to gather roots as well as leaves, berries as well as petals, in fact anything and everything which you feel drawn to. Always take care to make a positive identification and label everything *very* clearly as soon as you pick it.

Tie things up in bunches of the same, label and hang them up to dry somewhere warm and with a good circulation of air. The kitchen is not a good choice as steam from cooking will mildew the herbs and render them useless. As you bunch your herbs and plants, have a good sort through and take care to remove foliage which is not perfect. It is better to end up with a little that is perfect, than to risk loosing the entire lot because it is mouldy. There is no life force, and therefore no healing quality in poor foliage, so be selective and discard anything not in its prime.

Although this is called the Wort Moon and it is the time when the majority of things are ripe for picking, it goes without saying that certain other plants ripen at other times; like elderflowers and chamomile for example. Keep taking notes throughout the year and gather as and when the time is right.

It can be difficult sometimes to decide in witchcraft what is fact and what is unfounded myth, and one aspect of harvesting herbs which can be confusing is the story about the use of iron. It is a well-known saying that the Faere Folk hate iron but whether this symbolises the driving out of the 'small people' from our islands, or whether this comes from the understanding that iron affects some herbs, I don't know. The fact is, that if certain herbs and plants are cut using an iron blade, the properties of that plant are changed, rendering it unsuitable for use, either magically or medicinally. A suitable blade would be one made of bronze, which is a mixture of copper and tin, the proportions being 90% copper to 10% tin. Though this is expensive, it does solve the problem of avoiding the use of iron.

There is another method which avoids the use of *any* metal but with our enlightened knowledge of environmental preservation today it is not a very practical answer to the problem. However, just to offer further food for thought, I will put forward an idea based on historical facts. When farming was in its infancy, and people did not think as far in advance, crops of corn were harvested using a wooden implement which was broad, shallow and cut along one edge into 'v' shaped teeth. This was dragged through the corn, effectively removing the ears from the stalks; but it also pulled the corn right out of the ground by the roots.

Thinking about this method made me wonder if herbs and plants were originally gathered this way? After all, we use the roots of many plants, and it is in the roots that the power of the plant is stored. Obviously if this was the method used, then pretty soon any area would become stripped bare, and the hunter-gatherers would need to range further afield to find the food and medicines they needed to survive. This would fit in with the fact that people were originally nomadic, moving regularly between summer camps and winter camps and caves.

So does this business of not using iron have an even greater antiquity than we think? Perhaps it is a remnant of ancestral memory which has got confused with scientific fact and folklore until it is difficult to decide between. For my own part, I admit to using a knife, simply because it's practical and I do less damage to the plants. For those herbs which must not come into contact with iron, I take off the foliage with my thumb nail, and if it is root material that I need, then I dig with a stout stick. If the plant I require happens to be growing in profusion, and the loss of one or two will not affect the area one way or another, then I pull it up by the roots.

Yes ... this probably is cruel, but we only need to watch nature to see that the natural world *is* cruel. There is, however, a vast difference between thoughtless, vindictive damage, and being realistic. Whatever I take, I take with respect and consideration for the greater good, and I do not think that my actions are offensive to my gods. There are probably some who would throw up their hands in horror but they will never fully understand the Old Ones because they want everything to be always fine with the world, even if it goes against the laws of nature.

As I've said before, there must be a balance in *all* things, and destruction is only the other side of the coin of protection. We only have to think about the Element of Air, and how the leaves on the trees need it to survive. They spend a whole summer being ruffled by it, the tree itself takes in air and filters the oxygen to purify and replenish what we all need. That same Element of Air will quite happily whip up a storm and cause severe damage to those same trees and, in plenty of cases it will rip them out by the roots altogether. What is more, it will not sit wringing its hands in guilt over it.

I am *not* advocating or encouraging anyone to cause damage for the sake of doing so, but it is a fact of life that we sometimes have to destroy something if there is a real need. As long as we understand this and play by the rules, then a certain amount of destruction is acceptable. If you can find the things you need without doing any damage, then this is all for the good, but if you simply have to haul something out by its roots, then do so as gently as possible. If we loosen the soil around the plant first it will help. This is where a good knife comes in handy. Do be careful not to cut any root and afterwards, you might consider planting something else in its place. Give the new replacement a good soaking with water, then forget it. What's done is done, just don't waste whatever it was you took.

There is much to think about during the Wort Moon, and a lot to do practically too. It is like an antiquarian 'trolley dash' to make the most of all this bounty, and it would be impossible for me to advise about what should be picked, harvested and dug up. As I've said before, some of our choices are dictated by the areas in which we live, but it is still interesting to note which of the many different herbs and plants seem to overlap in their properties and uses. This means quite simply, that if we want something to cure a certain ailment, then if we can't find one plant to do it, we will find a substitute to do the same job. This is no doubt why recipes often vary from county to county. Nowadays we can all get hold of just about anything we're likely to need, commercially, because if we can't find it growing wild, we can always send away for it. Our ancestors didn't have this option and the original recipes were probably very simple, using only one or two ingredients if that was all that was available.

Rather than trying to provide a lengthy list of all the herbs and plants to be looking out for I will offer a very brief selection of recipes and potions, hints and tips, which will cover the very basics of a natural first aid kit for the average home.

Try to learn as much as you can about herb or wort-cunning, as this knowledge really *is* a basic requirement for any witch worth her/his salt. Some of these recipes have been discovered in old books, some I have had passed on from other witches, while one or two are what I have found to work by experiment and experience. They should give a basis from which to start to prepare your own stocks.

Just for a bit of fun I will include one of my grandmother's, which I assure you I was forced to take as a child – and survived. I don't recommend you try to recreate it; hopefully it's impossible to get the ingredients, and probably illegal if you did!

SAFE RECIPES
To cure a chesty cold and sore throat
1 tsp dried comfrey
1 tsp dried marshmallow
1 tsp dried lungwort
½ tsp dried mint
Honey to taste

Infuse all dried ingredients into a tea. Stand for 3 minutes. Add honey and drink hot. Take three times daily.

To treat a tension headache.
Infuse a few heads of camomile flowers or use a camomile tea bag in hot water for two or three minutes. Honey to taste if required. Rub a few drops of lavender oil on the temples or breath in the scent of dried lavender

To treat an upset tummy
A cup of warm milk with a pinch of dried ginger stirred in

Or Granny's remedy for feverish colds with cough in children, that included a brew of plantain, skullcap, dandelion root, camphor and turpentine, which is why I'm not going to give the full details!

Last but not least, if you are working with herbs for the first time, do take care when sampling any potions. Be absolutely sure that you have identified every herb with 100% accuracy; and do, *please*, invest in a good herbal which offers you recipes to follow.

All herbs have qualities which can be described as male or female, which is to say that some will have a calming, quiet way of working, these can be classed as feminine herbs. Others have a hot, rapid, more dynamic effect and these we class as male herbs. Some herbs have a perfect balance within themselves — but not all. In order to find a potion which will work in harmony with the body, it is essential to concoct something which ends up being balanced in both male and female aspects. This is a skill which requires a lot of study, and the novice is advised to stick to potions and teas which either contain just one or two herbs, *or* to work with existing recipes which are available in books.

The recipes that I have offered are safe enough for anyone to try (with the exception of Granny's skullcap), but always keep in mind that occasionally our bodies can react to all manner of things. Use common sense. Always try a small amount before drinking a cup full, and wait ten minutes to see if any reaction occurs. If *anything* you try causes any tingling or numbness in your mouth, seek medical help immediately, and retain the rest of the potion so that it can be checked properly. This goes for lotions and ointments too, if there are any signs of redness, itching or burning, run the affected part under cold water, and seek professional advice.

It is a common mistake to think that because herbs are 'just weeds' they are somehow not as strong as prescription drugs. This is a fallacy ... herbs can be *very* powerful indeed, so always treat them with the utmost respect. Do not make the mistake of thinking that if one teaspoon does some good, then two must be better. It doesn't work like that, so please follow recipes sensibly.

Another thing to watch, is how long a herbal preparation is going to be taken for. Many herbs which are perfectly safe taken now and again for a couple of weeks, actually become harmful if taken over a long period. This is because they leave a residue of their own components in our bodies which can subsequently build up in our liver and become toxic. Poke root is one such herb, fine though it may be in the short term, it is not suitable for complaints of a chronic nature. Read, study and ask advice from qualified herbalists whenever you can, and always err on the side of caution if you are unsure.

Besides using herbs as medicines and remedies, they can also be used in a magical way which doesn't involve ingesting them. For instance, if you wanted to do something to help someone build their strength to battle cancer, you would first find out which properties would be beneficial. In this case it would be a high dose of potassium. This can be found in red clover, bananas, horseradish and beetroot, among other things. Obviously it would be difficult to include these things in a normal diet every day, so I would make a felt image of the person which would be a good likeness with attention paid to body shape, hair colour etc. On one of the seams, leave an opening through which the appropriate herbs and dried plant material can be stuffed.

On a clean bit of paper, write the patient's name and birth date and as you fill the doll with herbs, get this bit of paper right up into the head; then continue to fill the dolly with the dried materials until it is well padded out. You may wish to include other herbs which you know would be helpful, but once you are satisfied with the contents, you can sew up the remaining gap and the doll is complete.

The next thing to do is to name it properly, and for this you should cast your circle of witch-power, which you should inject with as much magical power as possible. Do this by dancing, pacing chanting or whatever takes your fancy, until you have worked up a fine head of steam, then hold up the doll to the elements in turn, announcing who it is who calls them. Now, holding your charm of protection, call to the god and goddess powers to come to your aid.

Be quite firm about this, do not whisper and dither, you have every right to ask for this assistance, and tell them exactly what it is you want of them. Think about what you say, be specific, and state that you need this magic to be potent and to act from this moment on, and to continue until this patient (name) has no more need of the magic. You can request that the person in the doll should find ways of keeping themselves healthy, as they must do what they can to help too.

Now, cradling the doll in your hands, you should 'work' the magic of the circle into the doll. Dance, weave, chant, or sing (or all four) within the circle of power until you feel the power draining away. This chant (or charm as it can be called) should be repetitive and hypnotic, it doesn't need to be fabulous poetry, just something simple which you can mutter over and over again as you dance and move round the circle.

You may find yourself drawn to moving in one certain direction, in which case just go with it. Some would say that you should only move sunwise (deosil) and others would say that you should move moonwise (widdershins), and they can offer some reasonable sounding reasons for these decisions. However, I know from experience that you should go with whatever takes your fancy.

If you are so grounded that you can still decide which way to go, then you are a long way off being in any magical state anyway. In the circle these logical thoughts shouldn't enter your head, let the magic take you spinning once you are in your sacred, protected space, and the energy is stoked up. This is what the circle *is for*.

It's so we can step out of our everyday state, and enter freely into the realms of magic, where we don't *need* logical thoughts and rules and regulations. In fact, working solo is a lot safer because we only have ourselves to think about. Once we are satisfied that our protective sphere is around us, we can relax because it *is* so.

In group working, there can often be one or two participants who don't bother to check the circle's boundaries, as they are more than happy just to expect everyone else to do it. This causes a weakness in the sphere, which unbalances the power; and it is common for people to come out of group meetings feeling drained. This is something to be avoided like the plague, as it can take weeks to build yourself up again. This is the real reason why 'real' witches are extremely cagey about working with others.

If you are fortunate enough to find one or more person with whom you can form a tight, successfully working group, then value it. Once you have a group that works, I would advise against opening the doors to anyone else in a hurry, because the balance could be blown sky high, and it is nigh on impossible to rebuild it. This is one of the reasons why traditional British Old Craft (*true* traditional Craft that is) is almost impossible to get into. When we have something that works and gets results; when we have a group who can get onto their contacts to the Old Ones just by *being there together*, then the last thing that group is going to do is to risk blowing it just to keep the numbers up!

Be very wary if anyone offers you the chance to join them after just one or two conversations. Any group that opens its doors too freely is not doing so to offer *you* anything, in fact, quite the opposite. They may have sensed something about you, which they would dearly love to tap for their own ends. Keeping yourself to yourself, and well closed down will enhance your magic a thousand times more, than standing in a pseudo group and effectively being 'vampirised'.

Stand strong, but stand alone for a while yet, this way no one can spoil your magic.

There may come a time when you will meet someone with whom you can really work magic. At times we may find one or two more, which is a very special feeling. A coven can be a wonderful thing, but these days especially, it can usually do more harm than good to join an established one. Remember the words about egos? Well, most covens have a serious overload of them.

And this could harm your magic.

THE AIR TIDE
September—The Barley Moon

Almost everyone knows this time of year as being the time of the Harvest Moon and I don't think there is a time when the moon is more beautiful. On calm summer nights when the skies are clear, the moon sails overhead, glowing golden and serene. The fabulous skies that we see at sunset remind us that we are now well in the Tide of Air; this is a time of change and the autumnal equinox.

The long hot summer, in her moist splendour is overblown and sensuous; the vitality of the new tide, bringing a rejuvenation to Nature. This new energy is vital for the final surge which delivers the seeds to the earth; plants and animals alike are working hard again, using the strength gained in summer, to work hard harvesting her bounty. At some point during this moon, the balance will shift again with the equinox, just as it did in spring, and there will be a palpable difference in the air.

I know I am not alone in thinking that this is the loveliest time of year, and out of all the seasons this is certainly my favourite. Though the winter months are just around the corner, there seems to be a very special magic in autumn. Towards the end of this moon, we see some mornings start with delicate mists which transform and transport our world into a long lost time. We may see the hare again, and the beautiful hues of the hips and haws begin to decorate our hedgerows.

These misty mornings are a perfect time to work magic, and it is well worth the effort to get up especially early and perhaps make a trip to your sacred places. If ever there is an ideal time to seek the Horned God it's now, for though the power of the sun is waning, he is still a powerful presence, especially just before the equinox, when nature is building towards the final climax of summer.

Many popular books outlining rituals to celebrate the seasons, can be confusing, because of the way in which many people view the natural progression of the seasons. The impression some give is that our seasonal rituals and celebrations must always be *either* god *or* goddess orientated. One season being exclusively recognised as being aligned with a single gender. This seems very strange to me, because we must surely understand that there must always be a balance of both, to keep things moving and to instigate creation. In nature, at any time of year there is the presence of both the Ol' Lad and the Lass, just as we always have the sun and the moon around us, surely it is natural that we should feel the presence of *both* of them at any time we choose?

Think about what is happening in autumn; the corn is being harvested, the plants and trees are casting their seeds to the winds in the hope that they will take root in the earth and grow. These are just some of the things happening on the physical level, but on a magical level we could see it as the Earth Mother giving birth to the child she has nurtured through the summer. While the Horned God, moved by the majesty and power of this birth, is spreading his seed out of sheer bliss at the sight of the fruition of his husbandry. Throughout the spring and summer he has poured his ever-increasing solar energy into the womb of the mother, and now the magical child is safely born. Both the god and goddess are ecstatic, and the power of their energies is very potent at the time of the harvest. The equinox is the grand finale, the final rush of energy, before the life pulse begins to slow down again.

It is no wonder that so many myths and legends have survived in folk tales and customs. While spring brings a burst of new, creative energy, so autumn finally delivers the goods, so to speak. Now we can see and touch the fruits of the gods' labours, and we should take every opportunity to avail ourselves of this bounty, and indeed, it would be churlish not to!

There has never been a better time of year to start bottling and baking. Even laying apples away in the old fashioned way, if possible. On a practical note, have a go at making some chutney which you can put away till winter. In your Yuletide celebrations you can enhance your altar feast with this, and what a lovely reminder of the mystical days of autumn and the completion of the harvest.

As witches, it is only right that we should appreciate the completion of the year's cycle on all levels, whether this is an idea coming to fruition, or the birth of a child, or a bountiful harvest. The old wise women, the witches, the midwives were respected because they understood these things. They had learned their skills with herbs and magic so that they could help the new life they respected so much, to come into being. I think it is only fitting that those of us who would call ourselves witches today, should make an effort to learn something about the safe delivery of a child into the world. This is partly out of respect for those poor souls who were persecuted and put to death because of these skills; and partly because as witches we revere life, so it seems ludicrous not to know anything about our own species.

Most people have a basic knowledge about nutrition these days, and it is not too difficult to assume that a pregnant mother needs a balance of good healthy foods, plenty of fresh air and exercise, and naturally as much rest and sleep as she needs. Giving birth is a long and tiring experience as a rule, and it is sensible advice to encourage any mother to strive to be as physically fit and well as possible.

The first three months of pregnancy are often thought of as being a danger time, when spontaneous abortion can occur, however, the risk of this happening can be greatly reduced by paying particular attention to diet and rest. Occasionally, when nature knows that a foetus is not going to develop properly, a miscarriage occurs and, while this is a devastating loss, it is nonetheless perfectly natural. It does not necessarily mean that future fertility is going to be impaired, nor does it mean that subsequent pregnancies will not be carried to full term and a healthy baby delivered safely.

To reduce the risk of miscarriage due to an underdeveloped foetus it is vital that the mother has a daily intake of iron, folic acid and calcium. The first three months of a foetus's life are like a blue print for the rest of its time in the womb, consequently it is never too early to begin incorporating an added intake of these things.

A good way to ensure this is to make up a tea daily which should be drunk in small amounts throughout the day. A good pinch of the tea into about 300ml water. The water should be poured over the herbs and allowed to stand for about five minutes, but the water must not be quite boiling or the heat will destroy the allantoin in the comfrey. Honey can be used to sweeten this tea if required.

1 part blessed thistle leaf
2 parts raspberry leaf
1 part horsetail foliage
3 parts comfrey root or leaf
1 part nettle young leaf
1 part marshmallow root or leaf
1 part sarsaparilla root
2 parts yellow dock root
1 part allspice or ginger root
1 part cinnamon grated
1 part liquorice grated (omit if high blood pressure occurs)

Years ago, witches were the community midwives and there were many superstitions surrounding babies and birth. Some of these superstitions still survive, but medical science has advanced so quickly that the chances of the village witch delivering a baby are pretty remote. Even though it is unlikely that you will ever be called on in this capacity, it is still a good idea to find out the basics of midwifery. Your local library will have something suitable. Make notes in your journal, and include the herbs etc. As a witch, you have an obligation to at least know something about the subject.

At this time of year, the natural world is blatant in its display of abundance. Even just walking along the roadside, you will see the common 'weeds' turning their flowers into white fluffy pompoms of seed heads. The weather has been making perfect preparations for the planting. First the power of the sun throughout summer, warming the soil, followed by storms and showers, followed by more sun. The soil is a rich and fertile womb that will nurture the seeds until the time is ready, for the new shoots to emerge again. Even though we cannot see anything going on under the soil, the seeds will be slowly germinating; each tiny one developing everything it needs to grow into a luxuriant plant in a few months. Each tiny seed is as miraculous as any baby, because one carries the potential to ensure the continuation of its own type. The cycle of birth, life and death is perfectly displayed at this time of year, if we take the trouble to look for it.

This is a busy time of year and nature becomes almost frenzied about its preparations. Winter is around the corner, and Nature gives it all she's got when it comes down to trying to ensure that there will be an abundance next year. Seeds carried on the wind will be whizzing everywhere; plants with heavy seed pods will be buffeted by the increasingly strong winds until they burst. Nature is pulling out all the stops and the energy is almost palpable. Perhaps this is why many people find autumn their favourite time of year. Not only do we have a riot of changing colours to bedazzle us with beauty, but we still have the heat of summer and all the symbols of continuation.

The sun and the moon are telling us that as this month draws towards its end, we will once again reach an equinox. This is when there can be no doubt that we are on the curve which will spiral us into the depths of winter. The equinoxes can be a turbulent time, and we should not be surprised if it is. If you happen to be one of those folk who dread the equinoxes because they leave you feeling churned up and unsettled, then take heart. You and your magic are working perfectly! Like it or not this is a wonderful confirmation that you are indeed flowing in tune with the natural energies around you.

This, of course, is a perfect opportunity to work magic, because believe it or not, these turbulent times can be used to your benefit. This is also the time to take stock of your life, to evaluate everything which makes up your daily routine. Interestingly, we still use the phrase 'to take stock' - because 'stock' usually refers to a farmer's livestock. It is also used to describe a collection of provisions stored away, so it is a very apt phrase at this time of the year, when we recall that from ancient times, this is just what people did. Very few of us go through life without accumulating lots of unnecessary baggage, whether this is on a physical plane or the inner ones. Like we did in the spring, what better time to have a good sort out and 'cull' any unwanted items?

It is a well recognised fact, that most witches (if they have any degree of sensitivity) will tell you that there is a noticeably different magical feel to winter. We are drawn to doing things differently. While summer sees us setting aside our shewstones and cards, in favour of our outdoor pursuits, winter draws us instinctively to seek these things out again. In winter we are naturally inclined towards more secretive things: we actively seek that which is hidden. This is the dark-goddess energy of mystery and we should prepare now to embrace her. The following rite is designed to help us make this transition from summer to winter, or light to darkness, safely and with confidence.

AUTUMNAL EQUINOX RITE

The best time to work through this ritual is at the actual time when the equinox occurs. Though this is around the 21st of September, the precise time can vary to a day or two. The only way to be certain is to buy an ephemeris and check it out.

Because this is a time of rebalancing within the natural world, it follows that this is what we need to concentrate on within our magic. We already know that we are composed of the five elements of earth, water, air, fire and spirit. To be healthy in mind and body we need to try and get all these into balance within ourselves. The following rite is designed to help you achieve this balance in a gentle and natural way.

By attuning to the four elements of earth, water, fire and air, we are naturally creating a vacuum where the missing fifth element must come in as the equalising principle. This fifth element will be ourselves and as all the other four come together in harmony within us, we will come away refreshed and rebalanced. Be quite prepared for some turbulence as you interact with each element, just take all the time you need with each one, only moving onto the next when you feel re-settled each time. The results will be well worth it.

Prepare your sacred space at a time when you are sure of no disturbances. It is helpful to have representations of the elements. If you are working outdoors, then do please try to take the trouble to build a good bonfire. If you are working indoors, then try grouping several especially pretty candles together on a heat-proof tray—silver gives a lovely effect. For the element of air try smouldering a light incense, and keep some handy so that you can sprinkle more on the charcoal as you face east—failing that use a good quality joss. In the west try having a beautiful container such as a silver or cut glass goblet, and in the north perhaps a platter of home made bread and a vase of flowers to remind you of the earth's abundance. If the rite is going to be performed indoors, do have the window open if possible, so that you can feel the breeze against your skin.

When everything is ready, take a few moments to still your mind before sitting at the centre of your sacred space. It does not matter which element you begin working with first, but it can be helpful *not* to begin with the one you are most attracted to. We all have a favourite element, but to achieve a good balance, we must try to work harder on the ones we are *least* comfortable with.

Beginning where you will, breath deeply, still your mind, then focus on the representation of your element. Think about all the things that it means to you, spend a little time enjoying all the positive influences that it brings you. Think about the influence this element has in our world, let your thoughts flow, but remain focused.

Gradually turn your mind towards the negative aspects of the element. Think about the destructive influences the element can have on you. Consider the difficult aspects, push your mind to face the darkness of your subconscious. Go as deeply into these things as you can, go into the darkness even deeper, if frightening images appear, stand firm and face them. Soon they will lose their power, and gradually the positive influences which you visualised earlier, will diminish the darkness.

Let the pleasant influences resurface then let your whole being be flooded with this positive feeling. You have just come through the winter of the element, to re-emerge into the spring.

Follow the same pattern through all four elements until you have come full circle. Now sit a few moments longer, letting all the elements flood your being equally; at this moment you are the very centre of the universe. Do not be surprised if you have a very profound magical/spiritual experience at the climax of this rite. When you start to come back to earth, gently flex your arms and legs, rub your hands together, eat a little of the bread, and take a drink of the water. Through this rite, these things have become sacred, eat and drink them as such, before putting some outside as your libation.

Close the rite according to your own choice.

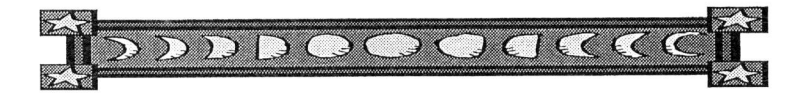

THE AIR TIDE
October—The Blood Moon

This moon needs no introduction, for who can there be who does not know that this is the month of the festival of Hallowmass (or Samhain pronounced 'Sow-en'). This is the old name for this time, but of course nowadays to the general public it is widely known as Hallowe'en, or occasionally All Hallows. Sadly even in our so- called democratic society, there are still those who hold extreme views, and who try to spoil the fun for many children, by calling for this fun to be banned.

To these bigoted, uneducated kill-joys I only have one thing to say: by all means do your own thing but please have the common courtesy to let others do *theirs*. Lots of people look forward to having a party and bobbing for apples but as for the American import of 'trick or treating' ... well I must admit to frowning on this because all it amounts to is a bunch of hyped-up children extorting money out of the neighbours.

The 'trickster' aspect, however, is a very old custom, known to witches as the Lord of Misrule. Modern children do not know that they are enacting a very ancient and tragic festival. For though the person elected as the Lord of Misrule enjoys egging on the revellers to greater fun and games, he is, in fact, the 'joker' king— destined for sacrifice at the end of his 'rule' at Twelfth Night.

To a witch Hallowmass is a special time, when the veil between the living and those who have passed into other realms, is at its thinnest. This makes it a time to honour the dead and, should we need to, communicate with them. This type of magic is known as necromancy, which has subsequently been linked to all manner of terrifying images. As a result, our ancestral feast of the dead has taken on a ghoulish reputation.

To outsiders it is not a time of spiritual significance. They do not see that what we do is out of love; instead they presume that it is a time for calling forth demons and ghosts. I suppose when folk have been brought up to fear the dead, then anyone who undergoes a ritual to contact them, must be doing dark and dreadful deeds. With this mind-set, anyone doing a ritual full stop, must be doing dark and dreadful deeds!

The name for the Blood Moon doesn't come from anything to do with dark deeds involving the dead. It comes from the reality that at this time of year, the villages had to ensure that they had enough food to last the winter and spring. This meant slaughtering some of their animals so that they would have not only enough meat, but skins for clothes. The fat would be rubbed down to make a form of suet, which is a valuable source of basic food; the thin fat would have produced oil for lamps and tallow candles. Nothing would have been wasted from the animals.

It wasn't just the produce from these animals which was taken into account. Any animal kept throughout the winter would have used up vast amounts of precious grain as fodder, not to mention needing bedding and shelter. It made perfect economical sense to single out those animals which would make good breeding stock in the following year and cull the rest. The retained livestock would have been well cared for, as it made sound business sense, while the ones that were only going to cost in terms of food, space and effort could be put to better use once slaughtered.

Our ancestors were a practical lot, and this would have been done with the interests of the people at heart. The animals which were going to be kept alive would have been taken into the living quarters to keep them safe from either wolves *or* raiding parties from other villages. The heat from the animals would have been welcome as a free source of warmth and added to that, the dung would have dried out as fuel for the fire - it was also be used as a type of cement for blocking draughts.

The people would have known that this was a make or break time for them, and provisioning would have been taken very seriously indeed. Provisions stored away now, could determine how many of the tribe or clan survived the winter.

Winters could be severe and much colder then; and it would have been natural for people to need to reaffirm their faith that the gods would not forsake them through the long dark winter months. The cold hand of death was beckoning through the mists, and the memories of those who had not survived previous winters would soon return to haunt even the strongest. Anyone old or in poor health would have genuine cause to be nervous and afraid. When we are afraid we call upon our gods to protect us, so it would have been natural for everyone to appeal for this help.

At this time of year we think of the Triple Mother as being in her phase as Crone, or the Old Dark Mother. In spring she is seen as the young Maiden, full of energy and promise and after her mating with the Horned God in summer she blossoms into the fertile and bountiful Mother. In winter she is once again as ancient as Time itself and, just as old people do, she retires to rest - ready to be reborn in spring, young and full of promise again. The Horned God, too, changes, for just as he is young and carefree in spring, he also matures in summer and gives all of himself into the fertility of creation. In autumn he sacrifices his strength, choosing to dwell in the quiet darkness of winter with his consort. His protection never leaves us, but we are left to live on our wits and our common sense to a large degree.

Many people will disagree with these views, preferring to hang onto the idea that if the Goddess isn't protecting us, then the Horned God *is*. However, 'as above so below' should be understood to be taken to mean that just as our parents or guardians love and protect us through our early years, before cutting the ties and watching us fly free, so do the Ol' Lad and the Lass. They are there to protect us if we need them, but we cannot expect them to magically do everything for us.

In the early moons we looked at how our amulets and charms work, and so it is with our survival. We must be seen to be doing everything which is humanly possible to help ourselves, in order that the gods will help us further. If they thought like humans, then I think they would be saying something along the lines of: "Well, if you cannot be bothered to help your cause, why should we?"

In winter, when the powers of the nature gods are resting, this is one of those times when we just have to get on with doing the best we can. The gods have gone deep into their mysterious realms to sleep and recuperate, and though they never desert us; it is a time when their need for rest should be respected.

Perhaps this is why for the rest of the winter, many of us feel drawn towards magic which calls the shades of the departed to us for guidance, rather than the Ol' Lad and Lass themselves. This is an area of magic with which many may feel uncomfortable, but one day we will all depart for other realms, so it is as well to become familiar with them, rather than fear them.

So far, all the magic we have learned has been quite gentle and safe, but just as the young man or woman must someday fly the nest, sinking or swimming on their own wit and merit, so must we as witches reach a point when we must go into uncharted realms, and find out if we sink or swim.

To celebrate Hallowmass it is wisest to go by your instinct as to what date it falls on. Even though the majority of people will recognise it as October 31st Eve, this may not actually be the appropriate time. I always get a very strong *instinctive* feeling about exactly *when* to do my rites, and this has absolutely no bearing on what the date may be on the calendar. I take note of how the energies feel around the dark of the moon at the end of October or the beginning of November, and plan my magical rite accordingly.

It should be remembered that the calendar as we know it today is only quite recent, it has been altered and juggled about until it fits into a convenient twelve months. This is why I have advised you to watch the skies and the tides for yourself because the thirteen moons of a natural year will not correspond to the calendar we use today. The chapter titles are only a guide, but try to follow the essence of each moon tide, feel the tide, rather than worrying about the fact that your Blood Moon may actually feel to be happening well into November. Magic is not bound by political or social correctness - remember what we said in the beginning of this book, give yourself some freedom.

To get the full benefit of the power in the Blood Moon, I would suggest that you allow yourself some stage setting. This is a very atmospheric time, and a little contrived window dressing will enhance anyone's magic. We all do it, however naturally we work and live, because there are times when going the whole hog is definitely to our advantage.

Whether we like to admit it or not, for a lot of us the festival of Hallowmass is one which (if people were a little more honest) actually concentrates more on the shades of the departed, than on contacting the gods themselves. Yet conversely, it is often at these precise times when we are not hoping to work directly with the gods, that we may find that we have made a powerful link with them. Nothing can be taken for granted in natural magic, which is why we have to expect the unexpected.

Night is the right time for necromancy - in the tide of the dark moon - and if this magic can be worked outdoors under the trees, then so much the better. A bonfire can be burning at the start of the rite, to show that there is still some power left in the waning sun. This will be extinguished before the end of the rite, so a large cauldron or bucket of water should be on hand, set to one side where you will not trip over it.

If you are fortunate enough to have a cauldron, then this could be filled with water, to which a small amount of your scrying fluid has been added. This would make the perfect medium for your conjuring, but failing that, your cup or usual scrying tool should be placed a little way from the fire. North is a popular direction, or West, the direction of mystery and spirits, however I know from past experience that if you conjure shades successfully, they will walk round the perimeter of your sacred space, not hovering in any particular quarter.

It is more important that you stand or kneel (whichever suits you) wherever you feel most comfortable. Quarters and directions mean nothing on the other planes, and whatever rules and regulations we follow on this plane is purely for ourselves. Have the courage to discern for yourself where you need to be. Once you have visited these other realms you will know just how different the universal laws can be, so always follow your own instincts. I must repeat that what I tell you is just a guide, offered from my own experience, but this does not mean that you cannot develop your own magical ways when you have gained confidence.

Besides a bonfire, a scrying bowl or mirror, and the means to extinguish the fire. I would advise the wearing of a long black hooded cloak or robe. This can be tied up round the waist or left loose, whichever is more practical. Set up an altar either on a tree stump or flat stone. If neither of these are available, use the ground, although you may like to place a black cloth down first. Because there will be a burning fire there is no need for candles, but if you want them by all means have them (but make them black or deep blood red!). Have a jug of home brew and an apple with some home made bread, bring plenty as you may find yourself sharing with more folk than you'd imagined.

The other item which you will have with you is your charm or amulet of protection. Refresh your memory about how it connects to you, and through which element it works for you. You must include something in your rite which works in harmony with this, in other words, your familiar or animal friend.

When you cast your circle with witch-power, do not forget to include your familiar, because in good witch tradition, your familiar is always in attendance (hence the name). You may want to place an image of him in there with you, but by now this should not be strictly necessary, unless he lives in some small container when he is not assisting you, which many of them do. If he does normally live like this, then do give him time to wake up before expecting him to leap into action. Do not feed him before he works, this can be his reward when he's done. At all times you must maintain a situation where you are the boss, a stroppy familiar is a nuisance to put it mildly! Don't ever forget that he is comprised of elemental energy, and this needs no encouragement to be naughty, I can assure you.

So, the feeling surrounding your Hallowmass ritual is going to be one of real working witchcraft, it is a highly evocative time anyway, but there is absolutely no harm in enhancing this with an altar, a dark robe or cloak and your charms and familiar in attendance. Once you have got the atmosphere: the flickering fire casting weird shadows, the wind moaning in the trees and the essence of the night all around you, do not think for one moment that you will not feel scared. Believe me you *should*, and between you, me and the gatepost, we all do! It doesn't matter how experienced we are, or how many other rituals we've participated in, there should still be an element of fear. As one witch friend puts it "if you are not scared, you are not doing it right."

This does not mean to say that you are actually going to come to any harm, but when the gods are invoked correctly, they are an awesome presence indeed. It is up to us, to stand our ground; this is not an arrogant stance, it is simply to imply that with the greatest respect, you still want to meet them, and that you have the strength of character to be a witch.

Hallowmass is our last chance to meet the gods properly, before they retire into the winter mists to recover, so make the most of it. Though they may never totally leave us, and in winter the Horned God still watches over us, he is guarding the sleeping Goddess from intruders, while he himself rests, so be respectful yet firm in your approach to them.

When you feel ready, cast your circle with witch-power. I like to walk the boundaries of my circle, knowing that my witch-power flows from my feet, leaving a trailing band of blue flame which grows and leaps until the flames curve over and under, forming a sphere all around me. This should be done widdershins (against the sun) and I always walk round three times, singing a personal charm as I go.

Next you should honour the quarters, those elements which make our life force on earth possible. It can be nice to greet the elemental kings of those realms by name, these being Ghob who rules the earth, Nixsa who rules the waters, Paralda who rules the air and Djinn who rules the fires. Though these powers are called the kings, it should be obvious that two of them are actually queens of their domain. I will leave you to work out which ones they are.

Now it is time to call the gods themselves, bearing in mind, that at this time on the wheel of the year, they are getting old and possibly less frivolous than at the start of the year. There are countless invocations available in books, and by all means use them if they ring true for you, otherwise speak from the heart in sincerity. You will be left in no doubt when they arrive to bless your rite, take a moment to welcome them.

I would stress, however, that the following is only an example and it is not taken directly from any older tradition.

"Dread Lord of the Shadows, lover of our dark Queen, though the time has come for you to rest, I know that I will be safe in your care, throughout the perils of winter. As you prepare to descend into the dark realms with your Lady, let us share this feast, especially prepared from the bounty of your union.

"May those whom I have loved, who are now with you in the shadowy lands, return this night, to share this celebration of life, be it a fit and proper reassurance that, though dark times are ahead, we will all once again be reborn with the coming of spring.

"Let my sacred circle be blessed with your presence until the fire is stilled, just as the sun now sinks to the earth. And in the darkness I will remember them and see them again. With the coming of the dawn, may they return to their rightful realms, refreshed and in peace, and may we all keep safe in your care, even though you rest with the Goddess. Even in sleep, may you watch over the creatures of the Wildwoods, until you return in the spring.

"In your honour do I drink of this wine and share this feast."

As you drink the wine or mead, and partake of the food, place a generous share onto a platter or bread board. This is called the dumb supper by some. This share of the feast can be left out for those who come through the shadows.

Now you can take up your scrying mirror, or gaze into the

cauldron. Do not be surprised to see shadowy figures moving around the perimeter of your circle. Simply wait quietly for them to enjoy the warmth of your friendship. When they begin to fade, it is time for you to also leave. Take a moment to feel the energies shifting slightly. The tide has now moved down into the Earth Tide of winter and your magical circle should be closed down to rest.

Thank those who have blessed your circle with their presence— not forgetting to thank those of the elemental realms who have helped to keep you safe. Invert the cup, as a symbol that everything is now closing down and douse the fire in honour of the dwindling sun.

When you leave your sacred space, you should never look back, so walk resolutely away and retire to bed.

"Lost in such ecstasies in this old spot
I feel that rapture which the world hath not,
That joy like health that flushes in my face
Amid the brambles of this ancient place ..."
                                        John Clare

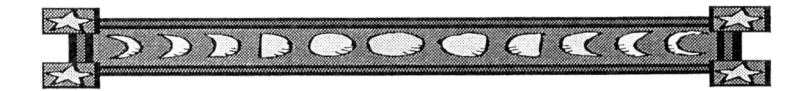

THE WATER TIDE
November——The Snow Moon

Before pollution began to change the climate, November was the month most likely to see the first snow falls. With the daylight shortening, and the livestock to feed and water, life would have been busy. The snow and rain would have swelled the streams and rivers, and it is easy to make the association to the Water Tide of winter.

Today, because of our modern life-style, the business of survival is not viewed in the same 'life or death' way. Our convenience stores and full freezers mean that the edge and urgency has been taken away from every day life. We may have a few wrangles over a hefty phone bill, or a few days willing pay-day to come, but this is not quite the same as the fears that people used to have. For most, November simply means that Christmas (Yule) is looming closer, and there are only X-number of shopping days left!

It may be more difficult to focus our minds on magic around this time, and we have to remind ourselves not to let these material worries over-take us. We must attempt to refocus on what this time of year *used* to mean, so that its full meaning can enrich us once again. This can be a helpful exercise in reducing the stress that creeps upon us as it can help to put life back in perspective. In a funny sort of way, this stress is actually in keeping with the old magic of this moon. It has been redirected certainly, but with a little thought, we can easily find comparisons between the worries of then and now.

One of the most noticeable things about November is the shortening daylight. We find ourselves coming home from work or school in the dark, and suddenly the roads and paths leading to our homes can seem more dangerous. We naturally find ourselves scurrying more quickly past parks and shrubs which we may have paused and admired in summer. The darkness can hold hidden dangers, real or imaginary and we are often glad to reach the safety of our homes.

The hearth light and warmth provides security and just as it did for our ancestors, we return to the comfort of locked doors and a good hot meal. Sometimes we may still gather round our hearths with friends and family, and even in this day and age, sometimes turn to telling tales to while away the evenings. It seems natural that these tales often include ghosts and gremlins and all things scary.

Perhaps this is all a part of our ancestral memory resurfacing, because long ago there *were* tales to be told of the frights which people experienced as they tended cattle and made their way home in the gathering darkness. In those days there were no street lights, and in the swiftly falling darkness, the mists and the falling snow, it was all too easy to sense danger around. In this quiet and darkness the presence of the old gods of winter loomed close, ready to terrify anyone venturing out alone. Even having the comfort of companions was not enough to allay those natural fears.

The energy of the old gods of winter can best be understood if we think back to our childhood. There are few who cannot recall times when, as carefree children we have gone off happily to play in the woods and fields, with the sun shining, and the birds singing. Without a care in the world, we have played and laughed as we wandered perhaps further away from home than usual.

As the days wore on, the games got sillier and sillier and at some point there was often a game of hide and seek, or some other game of chase. Who among us has not gone off to hide in some secret place, crouching, tense and excited, our hearts pounding, suddenly terrified of being caught? The fact that it is only one of our friends who is seeking us seems to vanish from our minds, and it becomes vital that we remain hidden. Even those among us who may not always have had friends living close enough to play with each day, have often played this game with a favourite canine companion. To suddenly dodge behind the trees, and hold our breaths as 'Rover' or 'Tess' dashes through the trees frantically trying to track us down. We remember the hysterical laughter mingled with relief when we were eventually found.

Usually these childhood games ended happily when everyone had taken their turns at being 'it'. The excitement turned to tiredness and we were content enough to make our way home in our own time. Just occasionally though, there were times when these innocent games became genuinely frightening to the point of us being quite terrified, and many of us may recall a time when we have run, screaming and on the point of tears at some threat, real or imagined.

Sadly, nowadays it is not safe for children to go playing far from home, but even so, the same excitement and the same feelings will arise even in the safety of a large garden or quiet corner. Even playing indoors can give the same thrills if dark corners and cupboards under the stairs are utilised.

In magic, we are not focusing on the real threats, so much as the feelings involved. Going back to the childhood games, try to recall the times when the game became a bit too intense. There you are, crouching behind a screen of thick bushes; it is a fine hiding place. You are a bit further away from your friends than you perhaps should be, well hidden, certain that the 'seeker' is not even close. A little way off, you hear your friends being found, but you are still well hidden. You hear them talking, all looking for you now.

Suddenly things go quiet, you are not sure that your friends are still close. There is a rustle behind you, for a moment you freeze, then again you hear a movement, it is coming closer. Suddenly you are genuinely frightened, you bolt from your cover and run towards your friends and safety, yelling that there is something coming after you. Your fright is infectious and without stopping to check whether the threat is real or imaginary, you all begin to run away as fast as possible, back to the safety of home, where suddenly the situation looked ridiculously funny.

Imagine then, what it must have felt like long ago, with winter and all its perils descending upon the villagers once again. The gods were closer then, and superstitions rife. To any innocent traveller out alone for any reason, the gathering darkness must have held many terrors. The threat of attack from bandits or wild animals was real enough, but the threat of the unseen force of the Ol' Lad was even worse. Even nowadays, when we are walking alone in some remote countryside, we can still experience the same feeling.

Who among us has not experienced that feeling which creeps upon us when we least expect it? The air goes that little bit quieter, and we get that awful feeling that someone or something is tracking us. At first we resist looking back, but as the feeling increases we cannot resist a moment longer. We glance behind us but there is nothing to see, and we walk on, unintentionally moving that little bit faster. Steadfastly we look straight ahead, walking faster, perhaps looking for a house, or another walker, and all the time the feeling of being followed is getting stronger. If we are fit enough we may break into a jog, and occasionally even run full tilt until we see someone or something reassuring. When we reach civilisation again, we might feel a little bit foolish at having been so easily scared. Without even being aware of it, we have just experienced the energy of the Wild Hunt.

This feeling of being hunted, and recognising that 'something' is doing the hunting is what our ancestors recognised as the Ol' Lad in his role as leader of the Wild Hunt. This energy surpasses any sense of right and wrong, for it is pure instinct and nothing else. We are not talking here about *human* energy, for we do know there *is* a difference. It is the primordial hunting instinct in the wild animal that we feel, and as we all know, the old gods of nature are as wild and free now as they ever were. However much our own society changes, the old gods will never change, and the instinct to hunt will never die.

When we encounter this feeling out in wild places, and when there really is no one out there but ourselves, we are in fact being drawn into the Wild Hunt. This is the polarity of universal law manifesting. Just as in summer we enjoyed the bounty and generosity of the Old Ones, now we are seeing the other side of the coin.

Modern pagans often recreate a 'wild hunt' with dances and games, and these can be fun. In a way they are keeping the old memories alive but they are pale in comparison to the real thing. You no doubt have experienced the genuine feelings as a child, and some of you may have experienced them as adults, and all that is needed are a few words on how best to deal with it, should it arise again.

The one thing to remember is that if the terror of the Wild Hunt should steal up on you as you walk in the wilds, it is a compliment! You are in the company of the Ol' Lad himself; he has noticed you. It is fair to say that he is hunting you, but it is not out of a sense of wanting to destroy; he is merely following an age-old instinct.

First and foremost you *must* double check that the danger is not real. If for one moment you actually feel certain that a person or animal really is coming after you, then you do not need me to tell you to run like hell. You do whatever you have to do to survive, and you do it double quick!

However, if you are certain that this is indeed the Ol' Lad, then for goodness sake enjoy it. Run with him by all means, laugh out loud with him, and even call to him to behave himself, but above all feel the *fear* of the hunted — for at *this* point you will be as near as you will ever come to running in the wild. The gods thrive on fun, they respect bravery and above all they are *not* offended by witches who show some spirit. As above — so below, that well known phrase is appropriate here. Just as the gods are full of life and spirit — therefore so should we be.

The Wild Hunt is one magical time that we cannot actually call or instigate, even with carefully prepared rituals. This is the time when the emphasis is definitely on the word 'wild'. The Ol' Lad, especially in his winter aspect is exactly what the word implies. He is wild, free and a law unto himself. He will appear and scare you, as and when he will, so we are forced to relinquish any ideas we may harbour about being in control of things. We must accept that these immense forces are *not* under our control, and the one final thing which is certainly out of our control is the aspect of death. When the Ol' Lad frightens us, he does not *intend* harm, but he is reminding us that we are indeed ultimately in is care. We can only place our love and trust in the Old Ones, and enjoy our lives to the full.

We know that November is also the time of the rising Water Tide. The earth is being bathed in the same amniotic fluid that cushions a child in the womb. The ground becomes sodden as the water tables rise and the period of gestation begins with the seeds slumbering in their earthy womb until the warmth of the spring sunshine draws them out into the world.

Unfortunately, Nature does often over-do things and we are becoming more and more prone to winter flooding. There is, however, yet another lesson to be learned here. Water, like all the other elements, can be dangerous as well as beneficial and if we decide to live quite close to water, then we cannot complain when we are given a demonstration of its natural and unstoppable power.

THE WATER TIDE
December—The Oak Moon

December is usually a very magical time for everyone, due to it being the traditional time for holding feasts and gatherings. Some deep ancestral memory stirs within us, and we naturally tend to meet, eat, drink and be merry. Though the modern version of these winter revels have become commercialised, as witches we can soon attune to the old sense of reverence if we give some thought to the deeper meanings behind them.

At some point in our history, mankind noticed the sun always followed a cycle which took it from its lowest point on the horizon, through to its highest point, and then back down to its lowest point again. We now know these two 'points' as the winter and summer solstices - hence our natural year is created and re-created over and over again as it has been for thousands of years.

Because of the importance of the sun for warmth, and to make the crops grow, its apparent diminishing was a time for real concern. In his innocence man no doubt believed that making offerings and even sacrifices to the lowering sun, would persuade it to return; equating human behaviour with that of the gods themselves. Sometimes a friend or lover can be placated with a gift and sincere words to persuade them to stay, and I feel it must have been this way with man's relationship with the sun. In this simple way, ritual was probably born.

I don't think we can still be in very much doubt that in the past, ceremonial sacrifice of live animals or humans (or both), were made. It is the remnants of these rites that have created the traceable rituals that are still with us today in our folk-lore. Rites like 'hunting the wren' are very old, and are believed to have taken the place of hunting a man. It makes sense to try and piece together what was happening long ago, in order to appreciate the full meaning of the rites we celebrate today. We know that at Hallowmass the Lord of Misrule was crowned 'king'. A king (or leader) who was willing to die so that his blood and semen (life force) could be poured back into the earth in the symbolic act of fertilisation. Incidentally, it is also a well-known fact that warriors/soldiers who are about to die, will almost always get an erection and ejaculate spontaneously just moments before their life-force is extinguished.

Originally, the king probably only ruled for a short time before being sacrificed, which would certainly mean that anyone accepting the role had to do so with great dedication. Because the king would no doubt have been chosen for his physical strength and wisdom, his prowess at hunting and his ability to sire strong offspring, it would soon become clear that to lose such a great leader after only a short rule was not particularly wise. There would have been a certain logic, however, in introducing new blood into the clan or village regularly. Perhaps (much to the king's relief) someone came up with the idea of electing a *substitute* king, who only ruled a short time, a king by proxy, who was sacrificed in place of the true king. In this way, the powerful leader could maintain his protection and virility for the benefit of his people for longer.

If our folk-lore is to be believed, this mock king, or leader, was elected at Hallowmass for a term of three moons, which took the end of his reign up to the winter solstice. Because of the grisly end that awaited him, he was treated with reverence, and had all the privileges of a king during his short span. Due to the solemnity of this role he was, understandably, allowed to be as frivolous as possible. He was actively encouraged to be as full of mischief as possible, and his job was to cheer everyone and lead them into as much fun as possible during the dark winter months. Thus the Lord of Misrule became the forerunner to the court jester.

As the centuries passed, these three main elements became jumbled together until we have Hallowmass; a comparatively modern combination of fun and fright, a case of humour and fear going hand in hand. No wonder it became a time for people to turn to the seers and diviners. At this time of year people probably wanted to look into the future to reassure themselves that all would be well, the sacrifices would be accepted, and the clan, and the earth would make it safely through the winter.

In our more enlightened times we no longer have the same fears about winter, and we know that the sun will start a new course to bring warmth and light again to us. For natural witches it makes sense to think of the day after the winter solstice as New Years day. Though the generally accepted date is now a couple of weeks later, many of us find it rewarding to do a rite privately at the solstice to attune to the natural beginning of the sun's new annual cycle. For this is the time when we can honestly say that a new year has been born.

In our minds we can divide our ritual into three parts, death, rest and re-birth. It need not be difficult to incorporate all these things into a magical working even though we are likely to be very busy doing other things around now.

The first part of our rite (the death aspect) honours the dying year. It is a time to look back on all that has transpired in our lives. A time to be thankful for the good things, and an ideal time to let go of the not so good things.

On the eve of the solstice, close to midnight, perhaps when the rest of the household has gone to bed, take a few minutes to sit quietly. You may like to have some magical things around you, especially your charm of protection. Look at it with respect for all it represents. Have a small orange candle burning (the colour of the setting sun) and as you gaze into the flame let your mind wander over all the important events of the dying year. Concentrate on the good things and, holding your charm, use your mind's eye to build these treasured memories into it.

Take as long as you like to enjoy these reflections before allowing your mind to reach further back into time. Now give some thoughts to those ancestral Lords of Misrule who died willingly for their cause. With an open heart, thank them for their dedication; let them know that they are remembered, even to this day. Honour their spirits in silence for a time. Do not be startled if you find that you make a genuine and powerful contact with them.

After a few moments, bring to mind all those things that you do *not* want to carry forward into the new year. (sorry but debts don't count!) And ask sincerely to be relieved of the burden of them. Let all the negative emotions drain away into the candle flame. If it is a tiny candle that will burn out before dawn leave it now (in a secure setting) to burn out — otherwise nip the candle out, as you say farewell to the old year. Let it go with a feeling of fondness if you can.

The second part of the ritual is very easy, for all you do now is sleep. As you drift off, imagine that you and the earth are one, and just as the earth sleeps in winter, so will you in a symbolic way, emulate her.

Check the exact time of the new sunrise and set your alarm to waken you in time to honour it. Try to relax and sleep deeply, rejuvenating your system just as the earth does. If you have any dreams make a note of them, they may be important as the new year unfolds.

When you wake at dawn, draw the curtains and let the light into your home. If you can, dress up warmly and walk to the highest point near your home. As you watch the sun coming up you will automatically feel inspired, the sun has returned again and it brings with it all your hopes and aspirations for the new year. Speak your feelings out loud, let your heart soar and draw happiness and well-being to you and those you love.

When you return home, light another candle to honour this universal miracle of nature. Red candles are traditional now, and as the colour red is highly symbolic, there is no reason not to use it. Family and friends will see nothing unusual in red candles burning around Yule, and if your beliefs are to be kept private, only you need know the symbolism behind it.

In Druidic times, the strength and power of the oak, and its annual return were no doubt equated to all that the winter solstice represents, and so we can still see why the month of December can truly be called the Oak Moon.

Though the majority of our festive decorations are artificial these days, we can help bring the natural essence of this tide into our homes if we have some fresh foliage. Try to bring in some holly and mistletoe, if you can get it. Any greenery like ivy will enhance the setting, and if this can be set off with red ribbons even better. The red of berries and ribbons symbolises the life force of the sacrificial blood, while the white of the mistletoe berries represents the sacrificial semen. Understanding these things helps us to maintain a reverence for these old festivals, whether we celebrate them in modern ways or not.

Magically this is a deep and quietly powerful time, but after the somewhat sombre ritual of the solstice, it is now the perfect time to relax and have fun.

Towards the end of this tide, you might like to explore the pathworking offered at the end of the book. But apart from doing this, set your magical activities to one side. It is a time to rest, and recharge the batteries, just as it is in the world around us. In this way we can truly remain in harmony with the tides of natural life.

" ... tasted the water of the two hidden springs which I worshipped. One of them bubbled out of the ground with a crystalline spurt and a sort of sob, and then carved its own sandy bed ... The other spring, almost invisible, brushed over the grass like a snake, and spread itself out secretly in the middle of the meadow where the narcissus, flowering in a ring, alone bore witness to its presence.. The first spring tasted of oak-leaves, the second of iron and hyacinth stalks. The mere mention of them makes me hope that their savour may fill my mouth when my time comes, and that I may carry hence with me that imagined draught."

Sido–Colette

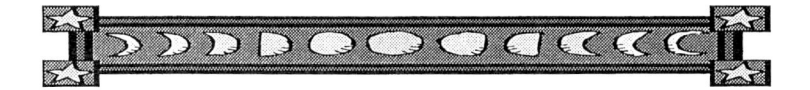

THE THIRTEENTH MOON
The Witches' Moon

Try as I may, I cannot find any records, either written or oral, which have a definite name for the thirteenth moon—unless as some say, it is the Blue Moon of popular saying. Perhaps this is because of the way our calendar has evolved. Nowadays we have the standard twelve months in a year, and it seems that the old moon names have been equated with these for so long, that the name of the extra moon has become lost in the mists of time.

It is difficult to even try to think of a name, because if you have been watching the skies closely, it will have become apparent that the thirteenth moon can occur in any of our calendar months. This thirteenth moon is always in a different month each year, and only by close observation will you know when it is, unless of course you have a sneaky peek at a lunar calendar, which will tell you at a glance.

Without knowing when this moon will fall, it is difficult to know for certain how our ancestors would have worked with it, therefore I am going to suggest, that you make it a time to do some special and personal magic. Maybe you will decide to think of a special secret name of your choice for the thirteenth moon, for there is no reason why you shouldn't.

Perhaps you could work with its magic to practice your astral flight, or you could simply honour it by making it a night when you reaffirm your dedication to the Old Ones.

If you have truly worked through these moons, then you have come a long way, and now it is time for you to fly free, and decide for yourself what to do. By now you should have an understanding of what lies behind spell work, and though there will always be those who would have you believe that spells are complicated, I think that you have seen enough of our reflective worlds to decide these things for yourself. Remember the old adage 'as above, so below'; this is what it is about. Whatever situation you create within your magic circle *will* manifest itself (one way or another) on earth. There are no rights and wrongs involved, but your *intention* is what decides the outcome.

Try to remember that some spells can take quite a while to work, be patient and do remember that if you want something to manifest swiftly ... then for goodness sake say so! Intention is everything, but we *must* state them clearly.

From now on let your instincts guide you, and though it is interesting to listen to the views of others, always decide for yourself what is right for you and what is not. You may decide that you would like to work magic with other people, and there can be a lot of enjoyment in this, however it may be difficult to accept their rules and rituals. It is a sorry fact of life, that there will always be those who simply want to follow the directions of others, and there will always be those only too happy to exploit this fact.

The life of a witch is not always easy, and there may be times when you wander a little way off track. This is normal, and it happens to the best if they are honest. If ever you feel that your magic is deserting you, or that the gods no longer listen to you, have the courage to attempt another vigil, with *no* preconceived ideas of what you will experience. What you need to know will be shown to you, and when you are refreshed and your sense of direction is strong again, then you will move along in another turn of the great spiral of life.

In these moons we have only touched the tip of the iceberg, and there will be many wonderful experiences yet to come, but hopefully I will have managed to pass on some of the essence of the old ways, enough to help you discover the witch within.

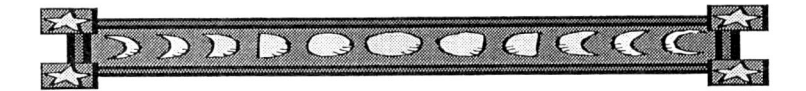

Epilogue

This book is dedicated to those who wish to live their lives to the full. So much has been said about life, the life force, and the spiritual growth and understanding that can be found living our lives as the witches we know ourselves to be. It seems only right that something should be said about another aspect of life, and this is the aspect of death.

This is a subject that often frightens people, and often it is something that they prefer not to think about. Perhaps this is because we have no absolute guarantee of knowing what really happens to us after our mortal shell has ceased to exist.

For those of us who have certainly seen people who are now in the spirit world, we have a degree of reassurance that life in some form does indeed continue, but even we cannot claim to understand a great deal about what happens in the greater scheme of things. In some ways, maybe we are not supposed to know too much, but one thing we do know about is the power of the gods.

It is human nature to have faith, it is a deep fundamental need which has been with us since the dawning of mankind's awakening. We should never feel ashamed to have faith, and when our faith is strong it is often the only thing that comforts us when we lose a loved one. How often have we heard people offering comfort to the bereaved by saying that the deceased has "gone to a better place"? We obviously have great faith in this better place, and witches have always maintained a surety that at the point of death, the spirit will move onto this utopia. Some call it the Summerland, others like to think of it as Avalon. Maybe the name does not really matter, *but our faith in it does.*

As witches, we understand the value of preparing to find our place in our Summerland or Avalon. We know that out of ignorance, fear is born, and so it makes sense to build ourselves a powerful image of where we will move on to. When these images are tinged with things we have been privileged to see on the other planes, and when we have felt the presence of the old gods for ourselves with certainty, then we can prepare for our final journey with an inner surety.

For generations witches and magicians have worked this magic, and it is something which should be undertaken as soon as we are sure of our faith and dedication.

This is something deeply personal, and is something which no one can else can do with you. Sometimes people who share a deep bond of love together try and ensure that they will meet again in this next level of existence. They do this by making vows and promises before their gods. Sometimes this is referred to as 'soul binding' but there is not always a name for these promises. While these oaths and promises may be made in true love and trust, they can carry a heavy penalty. It is not for me to say what others do about these deeply personal matters, but I would ask them to consider some things.

We already accept that we do not know for certain how things work in the afterlife, therefore these bonds may or not be fitting on another plane of existence. We cannot be certain that we will meet again in the *same forms*, one person may be handicapped in some way, or still needing to work through some spiritual stumbling blocks. In effect, one half of the partnership may be holding the other back, or perhaps in another life in another time, we may not wish to be bound by the bonds of this life.

There is so much that we still do not know, that it seems almost arrogant to presume that we can control each others destinies. Would it not be a much truer display of love to offer what we can in this life, but not attempt to tie one another in the afterlife. By all means make your plans for yourself, but do not try to bind anyone else into your plans. Leave matters to trust, what is meant to be, *will* be.

Keep faith in the Old Ones and they will surely keep you.

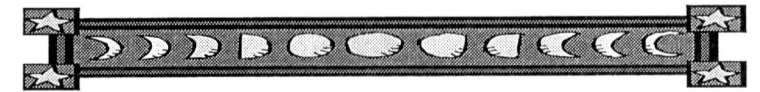

PATHWORKING TO THE SLEEPING GODDESS

THE PREPARATION

This is a quiet and very private rite that may be undertaken anytime, but the restful time of winter is very appropriate. If you can possibly brave the great outdoors do so, but an indoor working can be every bit as powerful for this type of magic. Wherever you choose to work, you will need a platter of bread or plain cakes, and a cup of wine or beer.

If you are going to work indoors it is a nice idea to bring a bunch of twigs and any evergreens that you can find, to your sacred space. This won't be needed if you decide to brave the elements and work outside, but as you will be sitting for quite some time you will need to wrap up warmly. It can be a good idea to take something waterproof to sit on, together with a blanket or sleeping bag. There is nothing beneficial to be gained from catching hypothermia!

Be sensible if you are going to be in a wood or lonely place. Let someone know where you are going to be, and approximately what time to expect you back. If you are at all nervous, ask someone you trust to remain close enough by for you to be able to call them in an emergency. Remember to have your charm of protection with you whether indoors or out.

If you live somewhere quiet, work this rite with a window open so that you might catch the night noises of an owl calling or the vixen's scream. The scent of the night is always evocative too, as is the sound of the wind in the trees. Before embarking on the pathworking, either familiarise yourself thoroughly with it or, if you can, record it onto a tape that you can play back at the appointed time. If you choose the latter, speak slowly and clearly, allowing pauses at the appropriate places.

Choosing a time when you can be certain of peace and quiet, create your magical space as per usual, before settling yourself comfortably. Pick a time when you are fully alert, or you may find yourself accidentally nodding off to sleep!

The path to the sleeping Goddess lies through the maze. This age-old symbol of our winding path of life. We can work the magic of the maze in our own space by walking or dancing the serpent maze dance. The ancient crane-dance is also very appropriate and not too strenuous, so even if you can only manage a sedate walk, the effects will be just as powerful. If you love to dance, it can be as expressive as you like, with as much movement and imitation of the crane as you can muster.

The basic steps are simply nine steps and a hop repeated over and over again. Have a practice before doing it for real, so that you get the feel for it. This will diminish the amount of concentration required to keep count as the dance will come naturally from the heart. The crane dance begins in a widdershins direction (lunar or anti-clockwise) with the nine steps and a hop. After completing these, you need to switch direction and dance the opposite way (deosil) for a further nine steps and a hop. Switch direction again for nine steps and a hop, and continue in this pattern until you have made four switches of direction.

Gradually working inwards towards the centre of the circle, you will find that by the time you reach the centre, you should be feeling quite disorientated. At the centre you should have a small candle burning in a blue glass holder; this is the point of return from all your magical journeys and often referred to as the sanctuary lamp.

As you follow through the pathworking, you should find that the light will actually be invisible to you at a certain point. When you start your return journey, you should see it ahead of you, like a distant beacon in your mind. This is your sanctuary, your safe point, for it symbolises all the safety and security of the circle. An ideal time to perform this rite is when the moon is dark, as close to the solstice as possible.

THE PATHWORKING

You have chosen to undertake this journey to the winter of the soul, and there will be nothing to sustain you but your own faith. Open your mind's eye as you sit alone in the silence and darkness. The way before you will be dark, and full of uncertainty. There are no guarantees and no promises. Depending on how you cope with what lies ahead, even the path of return may be hazardous. Look inside your heart and be sure that you feel ready for the task ahead. Take one last lingering look at the sanctuary lamp, before closing your eyes and bowing your head. Before you - only darkness.

In your mind's eye a scene is opening out. A vast and windswept open countryside stretches out in all directions. It is midnight, and the only light comes from the twinkling stars. Dressed in a warm cloak, and carrying your stang you find yourself walking towards a small wood on a hill a little way off. Owls call, and the wind tugs at your cloak. Tied around your waist is a small leather pouch but for now you do not seem able to remember what it contains. You only know that it is important. The wind is warm but powerful and as you walk it almost lifts you along, making the walk effortless.

Arriving at the edge of the trees, you take a small path, almost hidden by shrubs. It winds round the hill until it stops at the mouth of an ancient cave. You pause for a moment and look into the yawning blackness. There is nothing to see, and you have nothing but your faith to guide you. You feel a prickle of fear travel the length of your spine, but if you turn back now you will never know what lies in the darkness and mystery.

With head held high, you step forward into the inky blackness, walking surely and steadily. With one hand against the cave wall, you feel that the path curves and begins to slope downwards, but you walk steadfastly on. The sounds of the night are left behind and all around you is silence and darkness. The floor is smooth and the path winds gradually round and round, lower and lower, taking you deeper into the heart of the earth. There is dampness in the atmosphere, and the air is musty.

Suddenly you see a faint light ahead; it is only a glimmer but you walk on gladly towards it. The light is getting brighter and your steps quicken. Now you can see the floor and the walls of the tunnel gleaming with water; they reflect the light and the way seems much brighter. The silence is permeated by some noise, but as yet you cannot make out what it is. It seems to be coming from both in front of you and behind you—it is the sound of breathing.

Ahead of you the light is no longer increasing, and you walk faster and faster as you grow more and more alarmed. The sound is getting nearer; it is in front of you, yet behind you as well. The way ahead suddenly seems frightening, yet the noise comes from behind you as well. You feel confused and very scared. You have some moment's indecision about whether to go on, or whether to run back.

Pause ... *Allow all your deepest fears to emerge in your mind, for these are what you are facing now. The sleeping Goddess is within reach, will you press on or turn back? Have you the courage of your faith to continue the journey?*

Resolutely you tighten your grip on your stang, you take a deep breath and with head held high you walk bravely forward towards the unknown sounds. As you round the last corner, the sound of breathing gets louder, and the light increases. A few more steps and suddenly the narrow passage opens out into a vast chamber. Crystal clear water bubbles from a spring in the wall, tumbling down as a small waterfall into a beautiful underground pool. Here and there rocks jut out from its surface while the bottom is a bed of smooth pebbles in many different hues. To one side of the pool a small recess in the rocks catches your eye, and as you look towards it, something stirs within its depths. The deep rhythmic breathing changes, and the dry leaves in the recess rustle. Someone or something is stirring within the shadows.

Unsure what to do, you stand still and wait, feeling tense yet strangely exhilarated. There is a movement and suddenly She emerges, as old as time itself. Her matted grey hair hangs almost to the floor, her wrinkled naked body is stooped and lean, and the smell of death and decay surrounds her. In one claw like hand she holds a silver sickle, and you instinctively take a step back. Her fierce dark eyes hold your gaze, and without causing a ripple, she moves through the pool swiftly, to stand before you. She is taller than you imagined and instinctively you drop to your knees before Her. With head bowed you wait, trembling and clutching your trusty stang. Suddenly there is a swishing sound and you cringe as the silver sickle slices through the air, but bravely you do not flinch. With relief you realize that you have not been hurt, and after a moment you feel brave enough to look up.

She is still standing there before you, but now instead of being a terrifying wrinkled old hag, the Goddess stands tall and proud. Her lustrous hair is as black as the raven's wing and She is young and radiant, and Her face is full of love. Her penetrating eyes still hold your gaze, but the smell of decay has been replaced by the sweet scent of summer meadows. The air is perfumed with the scent of a hundred flowers, and Her exquisite face breaks into a warm smile. Holding out Her hand, She bids you to rise, and now you stand face to face with the treasure you overcame all fear to find.

In place of the sickle She hold a jewelled silver cup, full to the brim with clear pure water which She offers you with outstretched hands. You accept the cup and drink deeply. The Lady turns and dips her hand in the pool, then gently She touches the cool drops to your brow. A million brilliant stars seem to blaze before your eyes. When your vision clears the Goddess has gone and you are left alone to gaze deeply into the pool ...

... eventually it is time to leave but you remember the pouch hanging at your side. Reaching into it you draw out your treasured amulet. It has served you well all this time, but now it is time to return it. You carry the blessing of the Goddess now, and that is all the protection you will ever need. You place the pouch on a rock at the side of the pool and, grasping your stang once more, you take one last lingering look before turning and walking away.

The dark corridor is flooded now with a soft light, and the way seems shorter. Up and up you climb until very soon you emerge again into the open. In the distance you see your lamp still burning brightly, and before a moment has passed you are back to your starting place.

Rub your eyes, flex your muscles and enjoy the wine and bread

What you have just experienced is your first initiation into the Mysteries, and you know in your heart that you are a true witch. There may still be very much more to learn, and there may be many more magical things to perfect, but you have proved your worth to the Old Ones, and you will bear their mark forever.

Carry this mark with dignity, and know that from now on you will never walk alone.

May the Old Gods bless you and keep you.

The HagStone distance learning course

HagStone is a genuine working coven dedicated to preserving the Old Ways. It is their aim to help others learn these old traditions before the last threads of the true Old Craft slips away into the mists, or becomes buried under modern applications.

Until recently the HagStone distance learning course was only available via personal introduction, now, in response to the need for instruction about Old Craft, Fiona Walker-Craven has decided to make it more generally accessible. They do, however, still reserve the right to refuse an application under certain circumstances.

What makes HagStone different from other courses is it's flexibility. Not only does it offer a course for the solitary worker which is designed to take them through every aspect of a typical witch's training as it was learned long ago. It also offers the HagStone Unity course, for couples wishing to learn together to become a truly magical partnership.

HagStone invites you to join them in repairing the 'faded tapestry of life'; to help them to keep sacred that which should never be profaned and to restore it to its former natural beauty. HagStone promises to offer its students the chance to learn old witch skills, genuine spells, recipes, chants and magic. Learn how to live as a witch, and learn to do the things that real witches have done for centuries …

**Send SAE to Fiona Walker-Craven at
ignotus press (Dept HAG)
BCM-Writer
London WC1N 3XX**

Index

Air Tide: 12, 69, 79, 91,
Amulet: 17, 19, 20-21, 27, 30,
Autumn Equinox: 91-92, 95,
Autumn Equinox Rite: 96-97,
Avalon: 34, 123,

Barleycorn, John: 81
Barley Moon: 91-98,
Beach Working: 71-
Bees: 57-61,
Beltaine: (see Roodmass)
Blood Moon: 99-107,
British Old Craft: 35, 89,

Candles: 27-28, 117, 118,
Chalice: (see Cup)
Charm: 87-88
Chaste Moon: 29-36, 43,
Circle: 30, 55, 71, 88-89, 97, 105,
Cleansing: 26,
Crone: 101,
Culpeper, Nicholas: 64, 82,
Cup: 73-74

Druids: 58, 118,
Dumb Supper: 106,

Earth Tide: 12, 23, 29, 37, 38, 49, 69,
Elder: 44, 59, 75,
Elementals: 40,

Faere Folk: 39, 41, 82,
Familiar: 50-51, 55-56,
Fire Tide: 12, 47, 57, 69, 71,

Glamour: 32-34,
Goblet: (see Cup)
Goddess: 64, 66, 74, 101, 105,

Hallowmass: 37, 99, 102, 104, 116,
Hare: 48, 54,
Hare Moon: 47-56,
Harvest Moon: 91,
Hawthorn: 39, 41, 45,
Herb-lore: 45, 59, 61, 62-65, 70, 72, 80, 81, 82-87,8
Honey: 57, 58, 59-61, 69, 94,
Honey Moon: 57-67,
Horned God: 26, 64, 66, 74, 91, 92, 101, 105,
Horse: 47-48, 49, 53, 55,
Hunting the Wren: 115-116,

Incense: 45, 55

Knife: 30, 35-36, 73, 79, 81, 84,

Lammas: 81,
Libation: 45, 74,
Lord of Misrule: 99, 116, 117,

Maypole: 43,
Mead: 69, 72, 75-76
Mead Moon: 69-77,
Moon: 25,

Nature Spirits: 40,
Necromancy: 99-100, 103,

13 Moons

Need-fire: 41, 44, 45,
New Year's Day: 117,

Oak Moon: 115-119,

Pathworking: 126-131
Pregnancy: 93-94,
Protection: 13, 16, 19, 30-31, 32, 34, 47, 51,
Purification: 27,

Ritual: 77,
Robes: 45, 104,
Rowan: 47,
Roodmass: 36, 37, 39, 41, 42, 44,

Sacred Space: 31, 97,
Salve: 66-67,
Samhain: (see Hallowmass)
Scrying: 77, 81, 103, 106-107,
Seed Moon: 37-46,
Shapeshifting: 48, 49, 52-54,
Snow Moon: 109-114,
Spring Equinox: 36,
Storm Moon: 23-28, 50,
Summerland: 123,
Summer Solstice: 57, 72,

Totem Animals: (see Familiar)
Triple Mother: 101,
Twelfth Night: 99,

Water Tide: 11, 69, 109, 114,
Wild Hunt: 112-114,
Winter Solstice: 117,

Witches' Moon 121-122
Wolf, 12-13,
Wolf Moon: 11-22, 24,
Wort Moon: 79-90,

Yule: 92, 109, 118,

13 Moons